Leverage YOUR BEST,
Ditch THE REST

WILLIAM MORROW

An Imprint of HARPERCOLLINS*Publishers*

Leverage
YOUR BEST,
Ditch
THE REST

THE COACHING SECRETS
TOP EXECUTIVES
DEPEND ON

Scott Blanchard *and*
Madeleine Homan

FOUNDERS OF COACHING.COM

HarperCollins books may be purchased for educational, business, or sales promotional use. For information please write: Special Markets Department, HarperCollins Publishers Inc., 10 East 53rd Street, New York, NY 10022.

FIRST EDITION

Designed by Dancing Bears Design

Printed on acid-free paper

Library of Congress Cataloging-in-Publication Data

Blanchard, Scott.
    Leverage your best, ditch the rest : the coaching secrets top executives depend on / Scott Blanchard and Madeleine Homan.—1st ed.
      p. cm.
    Includes bibliographical references (p.).
    ISBN 0-06-055978-0
    1. Personal coaching. I. Homan, Madeleine. II. Title.

    BF637.P36B57 2004
    158.1—dc22

2004044945

04 05 06 07 08 WBC/RRD 10 9 8 7 6 5 4 3 2 1

S.B.: TO MY PARENTS,
KEN AND MARGIE,
WHOSE LOVE AND SUPPORT
HAVE NEVER WAVERED

M.H.: FOR MY MOM,
HÉLÈNE DE B. MADEIRA,
WHO KNEW ALL OF THIS

CONTENTS

FOREWORD

W hen Scott and Madeleine asked me if I would write a fore-word to their book *Leverage Your Best, Ditch the Rest,* I was thrilled. Why? Because I owe them so much—they introduced me to the world of coaching.

When they cofounded Coaching.com, a Web-enabled coaching, mentoring, and personal development service, I was intrigued. For years I've been frustrated by the realization that common sense is not always common practice. People tell me all the time, "Ken, I just love your books—I've read most of them. They make the complex simple. Your writings contain such common sense." I try to be polite, but I really want to ask them, "That's all well and good, but have you ever used anything I've written about?"

Just take *The One Minute Manager,* a parable about three manage-ment secrets, as a case in point. Since it's a small pass-along book, a minimum of twenty million people have probably read it around the world. And yet, when I visit organizations far and wide and ask peo-ple what they do and then compare their answers to the answers of their bosses, I get two funny little lists. The first secret of *The One*

Minute Manager—one-minute goal setting—is not being utilized widely. People are getting evaluated on things they didn't know they were supposed to do in the first place.

The second question I ask people is "How do you know whether you're doing a good job or not?" The number one answer I get is "No one's yelled at me lately!" In other words, no news is good news. Neither one-minute praisings (no one ever tells me they are sick and tired of all the compliments they are getting at work) nor one-minute reprimands (which end with a reaffirmation), the other two secrets, are alive and well either. The most popular management approach today is still "seagull management." These undisciplined managers are never around until you make a mistake and then they fly in, make a lot of noise, dump on everyone, and then fly out. Not a fun way to be managed.

I say "these undisciplined managers" purposely because Scott and Madeleine have also convinced me that effective leadership is more about discipline than skill. It's all about delivering on your good intentions. That's where coaching comes in as an incredible process that can have a big payoff for organizations. Why? Because if common sense is practiced, results are almost guaranteed. When a leadership or management training initiative is followed by one-on-one coaching, phenomenal results can be achieved. We've already proved that at The Ken Blanchard Companies, where we combine our world-class leadership training with follow-up work from Coaching.com. Why? That's something else I've learned from Scott and Madeleine.

There are three venues in which training can take place—one on one, one to few, and one to many. Most training takes place in a one-to-many environment—managers come together with twenty or more colleagues to learn some leadership concept. Then organizations, in order to get a bang for their buck, expect these managers to apply what they learned in a one-to-few setting with their direct reports. And yet, that is too big a leap for most managers because they have not yet integrated their learnings into their personal behavior repertoire. As a result, they immediately become frustrated with their success rate in applying what they have learned with their people. The interim missing step is a one-on-one coaching relationship where they can solidify and personalize what they have learned before using it with their people. So before learning received in a one-to-many environment can be applied in a one-to-few situation, one-on-one coaching is essential.

While these insights that I have gained from Scott and Madeleine are important to my organizational work and writings, the most significant happening for me that I owe a big thank-you to them for is my personal work with my own coach. When Scott and Madeleine started Coaching.com, Scott said to me, "Dad, I'd like you to have a coach so you can experience firsthand the power of what we are doing." When I agreed, Madeleine introduced me over the phone to several top coaches who she felt could effectively work with me, especially given Scott's description of me: "My dad is a 'slippery character'—he can persuade anyone that he's a poster child when it comes to behaving on his good intentions. So he needs someone he can't fool."

Given that reality (which I have to admit is more truth than fiction), I ended up in a coaching relationship with Shirley Anderson, one of the pioneers in the coaching field who had been Madeleine's coach for years (could it be that Madeleine and I have something in common?). To say that my relationship with Shirley has been a real gift is an understatement. Why?

I initially thought after taking my Scrubdown (you'll find out about that diagnostic tool as you read this book) that Shirley would try to fix me. But that was not the case. She treated me as if I was "already perfect"—one of the key truths you'll learn from Scott and Madeleine. Once I realized that reality, I could choose to change any behaviors that I felt weren't serving me. The key phrase here is "I could choose"—Shirley would not choose what I would change or even change me. She was my supporter and cheerleader for changing anything I wanted to change in my "perfect self." What a powerful perception—one that will be worth the time and energy you spend reading this book.

My relationship with Shirley has been a living example of a quote attributed to Bill McCartney, founder of Promise Keepers: "We are not in this world to compete with each other but to complete each other." Shirley nurtured a safe space for me (after all, I was already perfect and therefore didn't need to change) so I could complete my own "perfect self." As a result, I'm feeling better about myself than ever before. My three areas of concern—managing my health and fitness, not saying yes so often and as a result losing the "real Ken Blanchard," and developing an organizational system that works for a turbo-right-brain seeker—are all progressing. And without beating myself up in the process and thinking there's something wrong with me.

So read *Leverage Your Best, Ditch the Rest* with an open and excited mind. This could be the best book you have read in years and, in the process, help you to be even more perfect than you already are. Scott and Madeleine will propel you to what you yearn for—those things that are really important to you and how to get them. Thanks, Scott and Madeleine. You've made a difference in my life both professionally and personally. Let them do the same for you. God bless!

—Ken Blanchard
Coauthor, *The One Minute Manager, Raving Fans,* and *The On-Time, On-Target Manager*

INTRODUCTION

Snapshot:

A ten-year-old boy tears out of his driveway on his new—okay, hand-me-down from his brother but new to him—ten-speed bike. He has a wild gleam in his eye, his hair sticking out of a woolen cap his mother has threatened to staple to his head. He rides up the big neighborhood hill trying all the gears, feeling the muscles in his thighs start to burn and then his lungs as he puffs the cold air. He reaches the top of the hill and looks down at one of the longest hills in his county. He can see for miles around. He starts down the hill feeling his heart pound with the sheer terror and freedom of it. His eyes stream from the wind, and a crazy grin is glued from ear to ear. As he coasts to the flat at the end of the hill, big fat snowflakes begin to fall—he whoops and punches the air in a high five with some invisible best friend. He reaches up at the sky—look, Ma, no hands!—opens his mouth and captures an enormous flake right smack on his tongue. He closes his eyes in the pure bliss of a perfect moment.

A perfect moment.

Ultimately isn't life a series of moments strung together to create a whole story? And wouldn't it be wonderful to be able to increase the incidence of perfect ones? If someone were to tell you that things in your life were perfect right now, you would no doubt dismiss it out of hand. But you have to admit that everyone is *born* perfect. Created perfectly. A miracle, really, when you think about it. We all know this. That's why we cry when we see newborn babies. Tiny packets of extraordinary perfection. We wonder how maternity ward nurses can stand all of that perfection.

Then what happens?

Life gets complicated.

What about your life? How many perfect moments have you had recently—moments when everything came together and life was exactly as it is supposed to be? Of course you have perfect moments, we all do. But maybe they aren't adding up to the perfect life you envisioned for yourself. In fact, each year as we grow older it sometimes seems that instead of becoming better and better, life just seems harder and harder. Have you ever caught yourself looking with envy at a child or perhaps a college student and wishing you could change places with them? Wishing you could go back to a time when things were simpler?

What happened? What did you have when you were a child or a young adult that you no longer have? Did you have more freedom, more choices? Did you have less responsibility? Were there fewer people counting on you? Sure things were simpler and more carefree when you were younger. But what else was different? What else has changed since you had perfect moments almost every day? Has the way you view life changed, or has it stayed the same?

As coaches and consultants, we have had the privilege of working with thousands of clients over the last fifteen years. A few things have become clear to us. First of all, over time people's lives become more complicated. As lives become more complicated, they generally become more difficult. As lives become more difficult, they often become less enjoyable. Not that people don't enjoy significant aspects of their lives; they just don't enjoy as many hours per week as they did when their lives were less complicated. This is all self-evident perhaps, yet what is not self-evident is why this is acceptable. Some people get worn down, and many don't think they have the tools, resources, means, and support to take hold of their complicated lives and make them more enjoyable. Most people don't know how to systematically pull their lives out of the relentless confusion that has built up and make them—well—more fun. So they accept that life is a big slog. They keep their chins up and power through.

It doesn't have to be that way.

We have written this book so you can radically improve your complicated life. And we know you can do so without subjecting yourself to a life makeover, making radical and risky decisions, or spending any more money than you already have on this book. That's guaranteed!

In addition, we have built a Web site for those who have made a commitment to their own coaching journey. Coaching is a dynamic tool, and you are a work in progress—technology makes it easy to track growth. You can use the site to work through the exercises in this book electronically, keep a personal record of your work, communicate with others whose journey might be similar to your own, connect to related links, and ask us questions. If this is appealing to you, go to www.leverageyourbest.com. Your special reader login is Coachme and your password is now. From the generic log-in page, you will be able to become a member, customize your login and password, and protect the privacy of your work online. If the Internet is not easy for you to access, or is unattractive to you, have no fear, everything you need is contained right here in this book.

We are confident our book will work for you, as the perspectives and tools in it have worked for thousands of people with unique and diverse life experiences.

Leverage YOUR BEST, Ditch THE REST

CHAPTER ONE

Welcome to Coaching

What can coaching really do for you?

Snapshot:

"Things are good. . . . Well, they could be better. . . . Actually, I'm really fed up, and I'm thinking of quitting my job. I'm chopping away here, and there are no chips flying."

John, a production manager for a software company, is speaking on the phone to his new coach. He runs his hands through his sandy blond hair, noticing again how much less of it he has now than he used to have. He smiles ruefully at his vanity, at how it pops up at the oddest moments. When he was in grad school, he just hadn't imagined that someday he'd be sitting at an overcrowded desk feeling like he'd somehow missed a train.

He isn't quite sure what he signed up for with coaching, but he figures at this point he has nothing to lose.

"I had six meetings yesterday, and I walked away from each one with so much work I don't even know what hit me. I'm working late every night, my wife seems permanently angry with me, I feel like I haven't seen our kids in weeks, and the best people on my team are all about to quit because the workload just isn't easing up—it's getting worse."

"Wow," says his coach, "that sounds tough."

"Yeah," John says, "and what really burns me is that I seem to be complaining about the same things over and over again, and I just don't seem to be able to fix anything."

"Okay," the coach launches in. "Let's tackle this and see if we can't make some changes so that at least you can move on to some new problems."

John laughs and sighs. "Well, that would be a relief."

"Let's take a look at the whole picture. At how you're functioning in your work, personal and family life, and all parts of your life. We'll establish exactly where you are right now and where you truly want to be.

"I'll help you look through some different lenses so you have plenty of new perspectives. Once you can see your life more clearly I'll help you leverage some things and let a few things go and ultimately help you decide what actions you can take that will permanently eliminate reoccurring frustrations."

John likes what his coach is saying but still has some real doubts about getting this kind of help. He's never seen himself as someone who needed help. As far back as he can remember, he was a golden boy on and off the basketball court. He was always the guy people came to for advice. Why can't he do this by himself?

"Can you really do that for me?" John asks, excited but dubious.

"You're going to do it, John, not me, but I will show you some principles and a fail-safe process that will help guide you," says the coach. "Plus, I'll listen and nudge you toward what you say you want. I'll remind you of the many things you do that are working, and I'll keep your eye on the ball. How does that sound?"

A moment passes before John takes in a deep breath and says, "Good. Let's do it."

▪ GET A COACH IN A BOOK? ▪

Sound good? To see yourself objectively, to cut through the layers of accumulated mental detritus, to make clear-headed choices, and to take effective action toward creating a life that works beautifully? Whenever we describe what coaching can do for people, the inevitable response is *"I want a coach!"* Who wouldn't? When someone works with a good coach, they are making an investment in themselves like they are a hot new stock, and it causes them to take off like a rocket toward the destination of their choice. This book is our way of offering you the coaching process and the best coaching tools available.

Replicating the coaching experience in a book is fiendishly difficult because the perception is that the power of coaching comes from a relationship. While this is partially true, the most relevant relationship coaching addresses is the one you have with yourself. As coaches, we do a number of things with all our clients. We create an environment in which people feel safe and will grow. Then we use a process—a set of principles and a framework—that is easily repeated. Long after we have stopped working together clients often say, "I still hear your voice in my head." But we know that it isn't the coach's voice they are hearing—it's their own. Their own voice is now informed by a framework and a set of principles that helped them to gain clarity. Coaching helps people have better conversations *with themselves*; it helps people make better decisions about what is best for them on a minute-by-minute basis. Great coaches don't tell people what to do; they help people build their own personalized system to figure it out for themselves. This book can help you find a new mental framework and operating system. Call it new internal software, if you like.

WHAT IS COACHING?

*C*oaching is a big, broad term that has heretofore meant a bus (a means of conveying people to and fro) or a professional who assists others in the area of sports and other skills. Confusion abounds. Today a business coach can be anything from a Ph.D. in organizational psychology to an entrepreneurial fast talker. Frederic M. Hudson, Ph.D., founder of The Hudson Institute of Santa Barbara, one of the most respected coach training programs, came up with a wonderful way to describe what coaching does for people in his book, *The Handbook of Coaching*:

> *If individual adults can develop dependable radar systems for guiding themselves in and out of the never-ending maze of daily life, they can sustain confidence, self-esteem and hope. If individual adults can develop dependable gyroscopes for guiding themselves through the indefiniteness of their social experience, creating sufficient inner stability and outer constancy for living their beliefs, they will have surplus energy and courage for designing work and communities in our kind of world.*

The notion of having a personal radar system and a gyroscope is a compelling one.

The American Heritage Dictionary defines *radar* as "A method of detecting distant objects and determining their position, velocity, or other characteristics by analysis of very high frequency radio waves reflected from their surfaces."

Let's forget the high-frequency radio wave part and focus on the idea of being able to detect distant objects—in the case of personal radar, objects like competitors, layoffs, a change in interest rates, and changes in important relationships come to mind. Wouldn't it be great to be able to assess "position, velocity, or other characteristics" more effectively than you currently do? What about the concept of the gyroscope? More from the American Heritage Dictionary: "a device consisting of a spinning mass, typically a disk or wheel, mounted on a base so that its axis can turn freely in one or more directions and thereby maintain its orientation regardless of any movement of the base."

The key point here is "maintain its orientation regardless of any movement." Often we are caught in so much turbulence that we wouldn't know which way to orient ourselves if our lives depended on it. Our lives may not depend on it, but our quality of life certainly does.

Our world has gotten a lot faster, a lot more dangerous, and a lot bigger and harder to navigate. Like an automobile's on-board GPS system, coaching was invented to help people navigate our faster, bigger, more complex new world.

Coaching is an art of the soul, and coaches are artists of the soul.

Coaches help people to do the hammer and chisel work required, eliminating what is extraneous so that they can arrive at the things in life that matter most. In *The Secret Life of Bees,* author Sue Monk Kidd has one of her characters ask another why her house is painted bubblegum pink:

"You know, some things don't matter that much, Lily. Like the color of a house. How big is that in the scheme of life? But lifting a person's heart—now, that matters. The whole problem with people is—"

"They don't know what matters and what doesn't," I said, filling in her sentence and feeling proud of myself for doing so.

"I was gonna say, the problem is they know what matters, but they don't choose it. You know how hard that it is, Lily? I love May but it was still so hard to choose Caribbean Pink. The hardest thing on earth is to choose what matters."

Choosing what matters *is* hard. Choosing what matters has consequences—sometimes unexpected ones. Most of us don't choose what matters most to us because we don't have a framework with which to assess the logical consequences. We often default to the obvious or safe choice. Coaches help people construct a personal framework for consistently and consciously choosing what matters most. They use a process and tools to help individuals get to the heart and soul of the matter—choosing the best ways to invest in themselves.

▪ THE COACHING PROCESS ▪

The main goal of coaching is to help clients objectively see where they are (current state) and where they need to be (future state) and then to develop a plan to get from here to there—to go from point A to point B with as little effort and with as much fun as the law will allow. While moving from point A to point B may seem straightforward and simple, it rarely is. Many people have a clear idea of where they are going and may even have a plan to get there and still somehow never seem to arrive at their destination.

It has been said that the hardest line to draw is a straight one, and certainly it is the hardest line to follow. This is due in large part to the things that always seem to get in the way of well-laid plans. In addition to helping clients get on their way to achieving what they desire in life, we also help them anticipate and deal with the obstacles that may undo their well-laid plans. The coaching process helps people get from point A to point B and enables them to gain the confidence to plan and achieve greater things in the future, long after the coach has left the scene.

As you gain the ability to understand your own life and its dynamics, a side benefit will emerge. The knowledge you have of yourself will help you to better understand the people in your life. Imagine if you were able to understand more about the people around you—your boss, coworkers, spouse, friends, and family members—really understand what made them tick. There is no question that understanding oneself and others well is the key to improved communication, relationships, and results.

FIRST STEP: ACCEPTANCE

What made you pick up this book? If you want to fix long-term damage within yourself, this book is not for you and neither is a coach. If you feel you need a little tweaking, some focus, some structure, some clarity, then you are in the right place. There is one fundamental prerequisite to beginning the coaching process: *you must be willing to accept who and where you are right now and acknowledge that you are the direct product of every event that has happened to you and every choice you have made up until this moment.* Before you can make any changes and shifts, you must be prepared to tell the truth about your past and believe that you are basically fine right now. For some it is a leap of faith. That is what coaches do for people—accept where they are right now and don't judge how they got there.

 Snapshot:

Marjorie is on the phone with the coach she has been working with for three months. She has a huge whiteboard calendar on her wall marked with the Rollerblade dancing classes she just registered for, dinner dates with friends, and a monthly massage—all recent additions to the deadline-governed, goal-focused schedule that was already so full it was running over. There is no white left on her whiteboard. Next to the overflowing calendar is a photo of a lively redhead holding a laughing baby—she has a wide smile that makes others do the same. Standing next to them is a huge golden retriever that

also appears to be smiling. Marjorie loves the photo because she was always convinced that dogs smile, and now she has proof.

An account executive for a large PR firm, Marjorie hired a coach because, at age thirty-four, she realized she was rushing from her new baby to work and back without feeling any fun or fulfillment in her hectic life. She realized that she needed to regain some enjoyment, but the ways she used to have fun no longer fit her life as a working mom.

Now three months into the work with her coach, she is noticing a radical change in her quality of life. She respects her coach, who has been thorough and has challenged her to say no or maybe to the avalanche of requests and demands made of her. Her coach has asked her to examine what is most important to her and has helped her make real progress in restructuring her life. She is uncomfortable, though, because she has not been completely honest with her coach, and now she knows it's time to come clean.

"There's something I haven't told you," Marjorie admitted one day.

"Uh-huh," her coach responded.

"I was hoping I would have stopped doing this by now, but I just haven't, and now I'm embarrassed."

"Okay."

"Well, I don't want you to yell at me or anything."

"I wouldn't do any such thing," her coach said, laughing.

"Okay, here it is. I smoke."

"Well, I don't care if you smoke."

"You don't?"

"No."

"Oh." Marjorie was relieved. She thought she'd have to defend herself and the habit she judges herself so harshly for. Her husband hates it, her friends think of her habit as a misdemeanor, she feels like a failure, and now with a baby she feels doubly guilty.

"If you really want to smoke, by all means smoke," said her coach. "Now, shall we focus on your goal of setting up your system to be in touch with all your key customers as we'd planned, or would you prefer to focus on something else?"

The next day, Marjorie signed up for a stop-smoking group and hasn't had a cigarette since. When she mentioned it to her coach, he asked, "Does that make you feel good?"

"Yes," she replied.

The coach said, "Congratulations," and that was that.

Marjorie doesn't give it another thought—the topic has never come up again. It no longer matters to her.

But it matters to you. The reason it matters is because the only way you can change is to see yourself exactly as you are right now and accept that unconditionally. *The fundamental paradox of coaching is that you must accept yourself the way you are. Then and only then will you be able to make the changes that will serve you best.*

Self-acceptance is the key to individual behavior change just as accepting the imperfections of your spouse is one of the keys to a successful marriage. In his research, Dr. John Gottman of the University of Washington showed that a major reason long-term marriages endure has to do with how couples deal with personal differences and change. Many long-term marriages allow one or both partners to change over the course of the relationship, while many unsuccessful marriages fall apart because one of the partners feels asked to change too much. Ironically, successful marriages create an environment for change, while unsuccessful marriages create an environment where change is demanded by one party and resisted by the other. Why the different results?

Significant change occurs in a marriage only when the perception of total acceptance is already present in the relationship. As a happily married woman said to her husband, "I love you the way you are, Joe. I love all of your god-given gifts as well as your weaknesses. I love you completely, Joe! Now for god's sake will you change?" If a partner is not pressured to change, change is much more likely. Perverse, but true.

Coaching works in the same way. Coaches do not judge their clients; coaches consider their clients fine already and thereby create a powerful environment for their growth and development through change.

Yet, here's what most people repeat in their minds to convince themselves that they're a disaster with feet:

"I'm fat."
"I'm stupid."
"I'm a terrible parent."
"I can't do this."
"I am not good enough."
"Why can't I just get a break?"

Accepting yourself also includes accepting the circumstances that come your way. Hasn't everyone sat at their desk with their head in their hands wondering how something could have gone so wrong, only to have more bad news come knocking at the door? Bad days happen. Part of acceptance is to be able to view what is real right now without judgment, justifications, explanations, or blaming oneself or others. We are all affected by events outside our control; we can only control how we respond to them. Our ability to choose a response depends entirely on our ability to see situations clearly and accept the reality. Then we can change things.

▪ USING THIS BOOK TO COACH YOURSELF ▪

This book is designed to guide you through your own coaching journey. Though no two people have the same journey, the basic structure will look something like this:

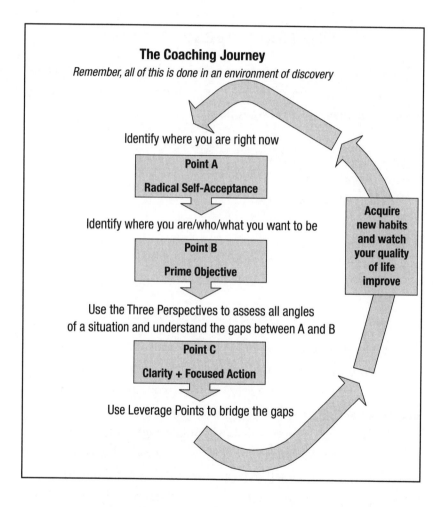

The Coaching Journey
Remember, all of this is done in an environment of discovery

Identify where you are right now

Point A

Radical Self-Acceptance

Identify where you are/who/what you want to be

Point B

Prime Objective

Use the Three Perspectives to assess all angles
of a situation and understand the gaps between A and B

Point C

Clarity + Focused Action

Use Leverage Points to bridge the gaps

Acquire new habits and watch your quality of life improve

As you are getting used to the idea of accepting that you are okay for now, you can get a sense of how to use this book. After fundamental acceptance of where you are right now, you identify an ideal end state—your Prime Objective. We will help you do this in Chapter Two. To get from point A (full acceptance of where you are now) to point B (Prime Objective), you have to have a good idea of what point A and B *really* look like. With a clear view of each point, you can get an idea of how to close the gap between the two.

■ THE THREE PERSPECTIVES ■

The Three Perspectives offer a multisided viewpoint that can expand the amount of information you use to formulate your assessment of where you are right now.

How do you see yourself?
How do others see you?
How do you want to be seen?

The Three Perspectives lead to the inevitable coaching question: so what now?

■ LEVERAGING YOURSELF ■

Finally, we offer the Seven Leverage Points. Over fifteen years of coaching people from all walks of life, these are the areas that have been the most consistently useful. If you apply yourself to using two or three of the Seven Leverage Points your life will improve drastically. To help you establish which Leverage Points will provide the most immediate impact for you, we have provided you with the Scrubdown, which is a self-assessment quiz. The Scrubdown, a time-tested self-appraisal, will help you to understand where to begin the job of addressing your multifaceted life. The Scrubdown is designed to help you to be brutally honest and the effect can make you feel ill at ease. For that we apologize in advance. But you don't want to build your coaching journey on a bunch of lies—there is simply no point in that. The questions you will ask yourself cut through the fluff and address the issues that are gnawing at you, whether you have been aware of them or not. The Scrubdown cuts to the chase by addressing aspects of your life that feel out of control, out of sorts, or off the radar screen altogether. Thousands have used the Scrubdown and find that it can provide refreshingly clear direction on where to focus first.

The Scrubdown is also important because it will guide the way you read and use this book, literally. Based on the score from your Scrubdown we may recommend that you start reading the book near the end or the middle rather than from the beginning. People come to coaching with different needs, some long term and others more immediate. Accordingly, the Scrubdown will help you understand the place to go in this book to get the best impact in the least amount of time. The book is designed to serve you in your coaching journey as quickly and productively as possible. You can follow our trajectory, or you can design your own.

The Seven Leverage Points offer you a guarantee: those who use them will experience a radically and permanently improved quality of life. They are:

THE SEVEN LEVERAGE POINTS

1. *Master* Your Universe

2. Manage Your *Gifts*

3. Get Your *Needs* Met

Continued

4. Cherish and Protect Your *Valuables*

5. Name and Claim Your *Standards*

6. Draw and Defend Your *Boundaries*

7. Eliminate Your *Tolerations*

We begin with:

1. MASTER YOUR UNIVERSE.

The first order of business is to find out: Where are you? What are you doing there, and is it the best place, the right fit, for you? What does your universe look like right now? We say your "universe" because all aspects of your life belong to you even if you do not want them. *You* choose what is part of your universe and what isn't. Your universe is your *context,* and coaching doesn't work unless you understand it, period. A sports coach works within a specific sport and game—your universe is your personal equivalent to your game, which means understanding the field, rules, and players. Then you figure out how your style, strengths, and skills affect how you are playing the game.

2. MANAGE YOUR GIFTS.

Once you understand your game, you'll need to get crystal clear about how you contribute to your team. The way you contribute is based on your gifts. You may be aware of what your gifts are, but chances are that you have lost sight of how best to develop and manage them. Gifts are a double-edged sword; they require care and understanding. We are seldom taught to understand them or how to administer that care. This Leverage Point will provide you with an opportunity to uncover or rediscover and, more importantly, to care-fully redeploy and protect the best parts of yourself.

3. GET YOUR NEEDS MET.

This is a concept that really goes against the grain. Most of us try to avoid needy people; we dread being one of them. A child says, "Mommy, I'm cold," and if Mommy doesn't have a sweater for her child or is unconvinced of the need, she says, "No you're not, honey; you're fine. It isn't that cold out." Come on, how weird is that? And how often did it happen to you? And for all the dysfunctional fami-lies out there, it is astonishing how many of us had perfectly nice, normal, caring parents—and they were the ones who told us we weren't cold, hungry, tired, or scared! The upshot is that we often don't recognize or honor perfectly reasonable needs when they are unforeseen, misunderstood, or inconvenient. This can cause untold havoc in otherwise stable lives.

4. CHERISH AND PROTECT YOUR VALUABLES.

The word *valuable* is a twist on *value,* a word that has become worn out from being co-opted by ideological movements. In fact, we will understand if you roll your eyes every time you hear the word, no matter what the context: living by values, family values, corporate values (and a fat lot of good those did us). Our aim is to shift away from the old word that has become burdened with too many meanings, so you can simply define what is most important to you. Valuables are the things you care about and pay attention to when it doesn't matter what anyone else thinks. When you un-derstand what is important to you—as distinct from what is most important in your corporate culture, religious community, social circle, or family—it can be surprisingly easy to spot why some choices you have made do not feel right even when they might "look" right. Once you understand this, you can make choices that suit you better and will help you to achieve your Prime Objective.

5. NAME AND CLAIM YOUR STANDARDS.

Whether you know it or not, you have an "operations manual" for yourself that includes a code of conduct. This includes what we think of as manners, etiquette, and professionalism. The problem, if you're over the age of thirty, is that the code was written ages ago and is probably outdated. A personal standard is what you expect of yourself and others. You will use your current standards to judge yourself and others, so they'd better be accurately informed by your needs and valuables. Clarity about your own standards can provide incredible relief from the judge who sits on your shoulder and provides a running commentary on your every move.

6. DRAW AND DEFEND YOUR BOUNDARIES.

Salvador Minuchin, a pioneer in family therapy, defined *boundaries* as "the invisible barriers that protect the integrity and rights of the individual." We define *boundaries* as "what people are and are not allowed to do or be when around us." The term has seeped from the world of psychology into colloquial use and has broad application in personal relationships and parenting. We extend the usefulness of the concept to situations in the workplace.

No one, no matter how well they think they have their boundaries covered, has this one nailed. Why? Because boundaries expand and contract as our world shifts around us. It takes a conscious and constant effort to understand and maintain our boundaries. Without them we find ourselves doing or saying unfortunate things to the people we have to work with or the people we love. The key to boundaries, once we know what they are, is learning how to articulate them and act in ways that produce positive results. It takes a little practice and finesse to draw bound-

aries without causing damage to relationships. You will see the
main reasons you fail to set and uphold your boundaries, and you
will learn how to hold and keep track of your boundaries as your
environment and conditions change.

And finally:

7. ELIMINATE YOUR TOLERATIONS.

Your final Leverage Point, a truly powerful concept, is that of tolerations. The late Thomas Leonard, a leading thinker in the coaching
industry, coined the term in the 1980s. A toleration is every tiny little thing that distracts you from what's important or drains your energy. Do you have any? You bet you do.

Tolerations add up to drag you down like too much luggage in a
crowded airport. We will help you to identify your tolerations and
eliminate them. Tolerations build up in life as naturally as plants
grow, and a plant in the wrong spot is a weed, right? We'll show you
how it happens and how to use the elimination of tolerations as a
way to build and maintain your quality of life.

CHAPTER TWO

The Distance Between Two Points

▪ ▼ ▪

What do you truly yearn for?

To begin the coaching process, we ask a series of questions that will seem repetitive to you. The experience of answering them may feel strange—even annoying. When a coach walks you through this thought process they provide accountability and don't let you off the hook. A coach would be patient and persistent with you, so you will have to be that for yourself. Make sure you have seven minutes of uninterrupted quiet, take a deep breath, and answer this:

What do you yearn for that has continued to elude you?
Write it here:

_____

Next question: Imagine for a moment that whatever it is, you have it. Now what? What does it bring you that you did not have before?
Write that here:

_____

Now for a big leap:

Let's imagine that whatever it is that you did not have before is yours. Now that you have it, what does this bring you that you did not have before? What does it look like? How does it feel to have it? Do you see yourself differently now that you have it? Do others see you differently? What about your day-to-day living—is it substantially different and better?

What do you now have that you didn't have before?

Write it here:

———————————————————————————————————

Okay. So now that you have that what do you now have that you did not have before? And as a result of this change, what is now true?

Write that here:

———————————————————————————————————

Continue to walk yourself through this process until you get the thing that you want most in the world. Is it freedom, safety, appreciation, truth, peace?

Write that here:

———————————————————————————————————

Many people in their initial answers say that they desire wealth, fame, or power or all three! But then they discover that the reality is quite different.

It is common to believe that achieving certain material goals will bring peace, or love, or something even less concrete and definable like happiness. What did you discover as a result of drilling down into what you want? What would it take for you to go directly for the end state, or that end goal, instead of squandering time and energy on intermediate goals that you hope will get you to the end state?

It is crucially important to understand the purpose and outcomes you will achieve by accomplishing the goals you have set. The last thing anyone wants is to reach the top of the ladder and discover that it was set against the wrong wall! Many people have very clear intentions and goals and yet have not carefully identified what all the hard work and determination will ultimately yield.

Very often people realize that the goals they have been working so hard to achieve are taking them to a place they don't really care much about. This can be a shocking moment of clarity—we hope that it happens for you early rather than late. The outcomes of your life today are the perfect result of the actions you've taken so far. Working through a coaching process will enable you to have a clearer picture of your life and the results it is currently designed to produce. Effective coaching enables you to plot the trajectory of your life and determine if you are headed where you want to go.

> "If you continue in your current direction, you'll get where you are going."
>
> —ANCIENT CHINESE PROVERB

Let's get more specific about what you want to create. It might feel small, like "to have a peaceful environment at work," or it could be huge, like "feed the world's starving children." At this point there's nothing to be gained from judging the size or scope of what you want to achieve. We will call what you want to create in your life your Prime Objective.

■ PRIME OBJECTIVE ■

In this section we will provide a template for you to get specific about your Prime Objective, lay out a preliminary plan to achieve it, and identify the people who will support you along the way.

To accomplish anything, people have to know what they are aiming for. How obvious does that sound? You'd be shocked to discover how many highly accomplished individuals are stumped by the question What are you aiming for?—in part because Prime Objectives shift with time, and we all forget that they need to be "reset" periodically. Now is your chance to do just that.

A Prime Objective is the specific and compelling goal around which a person designs their life. It is the end state you are aiming for in a particular phase of your life or business. A Prime Objective is not a vision of your future; it is a concrete end goal—it helps you focus your actions and efforts. For some this may be entirely based on a work or professional objective. Others may see their Prime Objective as something intensely personal that doesn't necessarily reflect a "practical" accomplishment.

Snapshot:

Marc has been a deal broker ever since he was a kid. By the time he was nine he had put together a matching service for babysitters and young parents, bought and sold used skateboards, and traded the costumes for his thespian sisters' fall show. He found buyers for sellers, matching supply with demand. He could smell a deal six miles away and, grabbing it, could make all parties feel like they were getting the long straw.

The day he made partner at a top real estate law firm in the city, he took his beautiful, funny wife (and the mother of their two kids) out for dinner at the hot spot of the moment. He knew which champagne to order, and they made a toast to this high point of his life. Marc had it all: family, work he loved, and a reputation as a deal meister, the ultimate rainmaker. But he was tired.

"I'm tired, honey." He saw his wife's eyebrow rise.

"What do you mean? You can relax a little now; you've made it!" She beamed.

"That's where you're wrong. It only gets uglier from here on in. Now my name is on the door, the big fat hole McCormack got us into two years ago is mine to dig us out of. Plus, three people need to be let go and now it's my problem; I've got to do the firing. Worse, I'm not going to get to do nearly as much of the fun stuff I love. Oh, and the real bad news is, the month at the lake isn't going to happen this year."

Nathalie was genuinely concerned now. "What is this about? Wasn't the month at the lake the whole point? Isn't that what you wanted? I'm lost, Marc."

"It is what I thought I wanted; but what I really wanted was to win. It was just so important; I didn't realize how important until I had actually done it. But now what I really want is the job of the guys I work for, and I want to do it from the lake with you and the kids."

Nathalie threw her head back and laughed a little too loudly for the ambience of the restaurant, a trait he'd always loved in her. "Oh honestly, you maniac, you've always been jealous of those guys. You just hate that they call you 'time card boy.' That's finished now. You're one of the muckety-mucks."

"Seriously, Nat, I'm sick of watching my clients close multimillion-dollar deals, deals that were my idea, deals that I should be making happen for us—you and me and the kids. I'm also sick of missing every single baseball game and skating competition. Listen to my two new favorite words: passive income. I got my apple in the big law firm apple bob. Now I want to make my own deals."

"Okay. Go make some deals then, baby." She was silent for a minute and then looked up. "Can we really live at the lake?"

W e have found that many people have spent years on a career path that is not taking them in the direction of their true aim in life.

Good corporate citizens who are individual contributors, managers, and senior leaders often spend very little time considering their Prime Objective. Organization members rarely consider the end they are trying to achieve because they are so busy focusing their aspirations on the positions they covet. We say this because we have seen many clients devastated when, after having lived a career, some for over twenty-five years, they reach the end and discover they were wrong about what their true goals were. As Lily Tomlin has said, "The problem with the rat race is that if you win you're still a rat!" Few things are more gut-wrenching than discovering that your entire career has brought you to an unsatisfactory place. This happens not because the aspirations you had for senior leadership weren't worthwhile, but because the reality of life at a senior executive level is often quite different from what you imagined.

The risk-taking entrepreneurs, the ones who go off on their own, are more often clear about their Prime Objective at the start, yet in the scramble of constantly creating, they can lose sight of it over the years.

Examples of Prime Objectives that we have heard are:

I want to retire at fifty and play golf every other day.
I want to pay off the mortgage on my house by the time I'm forty-five years old.
I want to have saved every dollar needed for my two kids' college education before they enter high school.

Are you getting a sense of what your Prime Objective is? It's okay if it's still elusive. Answering the following questions will help you to zero in on it.

➠ What are you passionate about? (What holds your interest, no matter how busy or exhausted you are?)

➠ What are you good at that doesn't even seem like work to you?

➠ What is crucial to your well-being? For example, being outdoors, being in a fast-paced environment, traveling? (See Chapter Six, Get Your Needs Met, for more clarity on this.)

➠ Does the thing you are good at have any commercial value? If so, are you currently leveraging that?

➠ If it doesn't seem to have commercial value, are you willing to go out on a limb to be creative and entrepreneurial about finding a way to create a market for it? (Did you know that the guy who figured out how to ship ice to warm climates created a demand for ice first?)

➠ What do you want people to say about you at your memorial service?

➠ What are you willing to risk or give up entirely to achieve your dream?

➠ If you could wave a magic wand and achieve your goal now, what would your life look like? What would it feel like?

This is the moment for you to plant a stake in the ground by putting your Prime Objective into writing. Don't worry if it isn't perfect—no one is keeping score, and you can always come back and tweak it as you gain insight along your coaching journey.

My Prime Objective is:

_____

_____

■ WHAT'S THE PLAN? ■

How have you set up your life to achieve your Prime Objective? What must you accomplish to achieve your Prime Objective? What little milestones must you achieve along the way? These questions often yield simple yet scary answers. Are your daily, weekly, monthly, and yearly actions taking you on a path that will result in what you want?

We've heard people nearing middle age who are considering going for an additional degree say, "But I'll be so old when I finally have it." True, and the answer to that is always: you'll be five years older in five years no matter what you do, but consider the fact that you can be five years older with a degree or without one. In order to achieve a Prime Objective of retiring at age sixty and moving to the beach in Florida, you must create enough wealth to be able to afford to stop working and move to Florida. And if you are really serious about retiring in Florida, you must start preparing for this Prime Objective long before you get into your fifties. Hope is not an effective tool in achieving the Prime Objective, but *planning* is.

We learned a lot from a friend of ours named Paul who is a successful headhunter in the hospitality industry. Paul has seen it all in his years as a headhunter. He has heard more stories than he can stand from job candidates who want more money and greater levels of responsibility. From where he sits, most of his candidates do not see what he sees on paper. What he sees is that most of them are lucky to have the jobs they have and have certainly not demonstrated what is necessary to warrant the more lucrative, higher quality positions they desire.

One day Paul stopped a candidate midsentence and said, "Let me tell you what I see in this résumé. I placed you in your last two positions, and if I were to project the future of your career based on what I see in the past ten years, it's not a pretty picture. You say you want to earn more money and have greater responsibility, yet your record indicates that like so many other chefs, you have trouble getting along with people. Just about every time we sit down and talk about where you want to go in your work, we end up talking about how you were unable to get along with the executive chef, the food and beverage manager, or someone else in your workplace. It's always someone else's fault. When I look at your résumé and listen to your story, I can see exactly how your career will turn out. Here is how things are going to happen: you will continue to change jobs every year or two and will most likely become a bitter and frustrated assistant chef who never seems to find success as an executive chef."

The candidate was shocked, and Paul realized he had stepped over the line, but for some reason the guy did not get up and leave. Instead he sat there in disbelief at what he had heard. Finally he asked, "Is my career really that predictable?"

Paul took a deep breath and said, "Yes. I meet with hundreds of candidates a year and can literally tell where their careers are going just by looking at their résumés. Of course, if you don't want your career to end in disappointment, maybe we should talk about what you can do differently in your next job to make sure you're not sitting here again in two years."

From that point on, Paul changed the way he ran his headhunting practice. He now sits down with his new candidates and asks them to look at their résumé, plot their current trajectory, and decide if it is the correct path for them. He is coaching them, in effect, to identify the obstacles they themselves put in the way of achieving their Prime Objective.

What actions could you be taking now that had not occurred to you before?

A man—a true believer—on his knees in despair is begging God. "God," he says, "my sweetie, my darling, she needs medicine, and I do not have the money. Please, God, please, let me win the lottery."

The next week, he is back on his knees. "God, my God, the loan has come due, I don't have the money. Please, I am begging on my knees, please let me win the lottery."

The man prays and prays to no avail. He becomes more and more frustrated and angry with God for not answering his prayers. Again, a week later, he is back at it. "God, please listen to me. I'm desperate, please; please let me win the—"

He is interrupted by an impatient voice booming from above: "Son, help me out—buy a ticket."

■ WE PLAN, GOD LAUGHS ■

It is true, most short- and long-term plans do not work out the way we thought they would. We have not seen a single plan that worked . . . perfectly that is. For years Ken Blanchard has said that life is what happens when you are planning on doing something else.

So does this mean you should not create plans? Absolutely not. Good planning is critical to achieving your goals in life. It is just really important to maintain a realistic perspective when it comes to planning. The most successful people we have observed in life have the capacity to be fully committed to their plans and yet flexible enough to accept certain realities as they occur. When you have a plan, you will end up with something close or better than your plan. Some invest time and energy in creating well-calculated plans to achieve their goals, while others do minimal planning and then just fling themselves into action. Regardless of the approach, extensive planning or light planning, a good plan includes a purposeful end and clear, specific, and definable actions to take.

Action provides us with important feedback that tells us whether or not our actions and approach will help us achieve our Prime Objective. Action begets action; the biggest mistake many people make is doing nothing. They are always "getting ready" to act differently, to take new paths, to reach for something significant. But getting ready, or merely devising a plan, doesn't count as much as setting that plan into action. Only action creates movement, and if you aren't moving, you are standing in the same place. To our knowledge, intention or thought has never moved a single person off the dime.

When we take action, we get information and messages. Some information is good news, as in "Keep going, you're on the right track, this will yield what you are after." The bad news comes in two categories: problems and insurmountable obstacles. Unfortunately, problems are hard to distinguish from insurmountable obstacles. This is when it is important to be clear about your needs and valuables because knowing them will help you distinguish between problems you can solve, risks you are willing to take, and what you are willing and not willing to give up. Human beings are extraordinarily resilient, and if the Prime Objective is compelling enough, they will put up with deprivation and suffering.

How do you know if the actions you are planning to take are the right ones? You don't really. You can do your homework, talk to successful people who have achieved what you are seeking to achieve, read up on the subject, but ultimately you are making an informed guess.

One way to refine your guess is to create a backward plan. Madeleine learned the technique of backward planning from her first coach, a thought leader in the industry, Henry Kimsey-House.

The very simple premise of backward planning is that you define your Prime Objective, or a big goal that will move you toward your Prime Objective, and assign it a date. As Henry said, "A goal without a date is a dream." Then you need to figure out the very next-to-last thing that needs to happen before your goal is met and the time frame for that. Then ask, What would need to happen before that? And before that?

Here is an example of a backward plan:

Goal: By (three to five years out, with exact date) I will be a practicing attorney in a law firm.

Six months prior I will have graduated from law school with a J.D. degree.

In summer of _____ **(one year prior)** I will be employed as a summer intern at the Jones, Smith & Everyman Law firm.

By January (or six months prior) I will have secured an internship with a law firm that meets specific criteria.

As of (six months prior) I will be in the top 25 percent of my class through the first year of law school.

By spring of (one year prior) I will have been accepted to a prestigious law school.

By fall (six months prior) I will have taken the LSAT test and scored at or above the 80th percentile.

It starts with a clear and tangible Prime Objective, to be practicing law. The logic required to do a backward plan is to start with the end in mind and then ask yourself the following question: to accomplish my goal, what has to happen? And so the process goes until you reach the present.

Backward planning is a simple tool that very few people know about and use.

My Backward Plan

By _____ I will have achieved _____.
    (date)   (Prime Objective)

Just prior to that _____ I will need to have done _____
                        (date)   (milestone)

_____.

And before that can happen, by _____ I will need to have accomplished
                                      (date)

_____.
(milestone)

To enable the next step, by _____ I will need to have_____
                                  (date)   (milestone)

_____ in place.

By _____ I will have done _____
    (date)   (milestone)

_____.

By _____ I will have done _____
    (date)   (milestone)

_____.

Today (or tomorrow) I will _____.
                                (milestone)

Now that you have a clear Prime Objective and the beginnings of your plan to get there, you can really get cooking with the coaching process. We say "the beginnings" because your plan will alter as you take action and gather information. At least now you have a clear picture of where you are headed—a critical foundation to achieving what you want. However, life is a journey that must be lived day by day. For this reason, our process will now shift gears from the abstract and the future to the concrete and the present. While striving for things in the future gives us direction, our daily actions are the only things we can really control.

To help get a sense of your daily life, complete a self-assessment, the Scrubdown, on page 32. Coaches have used this method of self-assessment for more than a decade. Simply answer *true* or *false* to each statement. If the statement does apply to you, circle T for *true*. If you are not sure, ask yourself, "Is this true 80 percent of the time?" If the answer to that is yes, go ahead and circle T. You have everything to gain, and nothing to lose, by being brutally honest with yourself. Many highly successful people have a surprisingly low total of *true* answers at first.

For you to be truly honest with yourself, you need to remember the first requirement of creating your personal coaching environment. We suspect you may have forgotten it, so here it is again—*you are a perfect sum of everything that has happened to you up to the present moment.* Some choices were wise and good, others were made without enough information, and a few were simply made by default. All of that is merely history now. The point of the Scrubdown is to provide you with information and feedback about the choices you have made up to this point in time and provide you with some potential areas of focus for moving forward. You will find some things you will want to start doing, some things you will want to stop, and some things you will want to continue. The Scrubdown provides clarity about what you want to leverage in your life and what you can ditch.

The key to a higher quality of life is learning how to avoid all the predictable crap and to build hedges against the rest. No one can prevent the occasional disaster, but wouldn't it be good to know that if you did end up in the hospital, someone would help take care of your kids, your house, your dog, your work? Instead of living in a house of cards that can fall down in the slightest breeze, you need a life as solid as a brick house that can withstand a good stiff wind.

The Scrubdown

1. I am aware how people I work with see me .... T F
2. I know whom in my life to go to with what issue .... T F
3. I step back and reassess when I feel overwhelmed .... T F
4. I don't obsess over things that I know do not matter .... T F
5. I have found a way to use the best of myself in what I do every day .... T F
6. I know when I am expecting too much of myself .... T F
7. I do not spend time with people I dislike .... T F
8. I do not "lose time" because of lost items, lack of equipment, or poor
   organization .... T F
9. My self-image doesn't shift dramatically in different environments .... T F
10. If I have a problem or complaint, I speak with the appropriate person quickly .... T F
11. I know when I am getting overstressed .... T F
12. I know what is most important to me .... T F
13. I do not covet what other people have .... T F
14. I don't resent my own rules .... T F
15. I am rarely late .... T F
16. I know what I need to do to appear "well put together" and it requires
    little thought .... T F
17. I get consistent feedback from important people in my life .... T F
18. I have mastered building relationships .... T F
19. I know how to ask for what I need appropriately .... T F
20. I surround myself with things that give me joy .... T F
21. I am comfortable acknowledging my strongest attributes .... T F
22. I have achieved a comfort level with my "to-do" list .... T F
23. I say what I mean and mean what I say .... T F
24. I am at peace in my home/office .... T F
25. I understand how to relate with people and set them at ease .... T F
26. I bring out the best in people .... T F
27. I have all the love and appreciation I need .... T F
28. I surround myself with people I care about .... T F
29. I know what I am great at .... T F
30. I don't lose sleep over any promises I have made .... T F
31. I say no when I must without guilt .... T F
32. I am comfortable with the way my body looks and feels .... T F
33. I know what I can expect of myself .... T F
34. I express an interest in others .... T F
35. The important people in my life treat me the way I want to be treated .... T F
36. I know what brings out the best in me .... T F
37. I never pretend to be less smart/educated than I am .... T F
38. I know what promises I have made and have a plan to deliver on all of them .... T F
39. I get enough rest and relaxation .... T F
40. I have a time and task management system that works for me .... T F

For those of you with access to the Internet, go to www.lever ageyourbest.com and follow the directions on the site. If you take the Scrubdown on the Internet, the scoring will be automatic once you submit your responses. In a matter of minutes you will receive your Scrubdown results.

▪ SCORECARD ▪

Interpreting the Scrubdown is accomplished in two different ways. The first way is item by item. To do this, simply ask yourself the following question:

What one or two *false* answers did you really want to be *true*?
Record your answers below:

1. _____

2. _____

You may find that the individual items on the Scrubdown point out gaps in your life that you are not satisfied with. For example, what if you answered *false* to the statement "I do not spend time with people I dislike"? It may cause you to realize that your current job requires that you spend time with negative people and this is not acceptable. It may cause, in an instant, a realization that life is too short to hate your job and now may be as good a time as ever to start actually doing something about getting a new job, a new career, going back to school, or simply making a change in your environment, like drawing some boundaries.

The second way to use the Scrubdown is to discover the broader pattern that results from your answers. To do this, go down your questionnaire and circle the numbers of the statements that were *false* on the grid on the next page. When you have finished, add the

1	2	5	3	4	6	7	8	
9	10	13	11	12	14	15	16	
17	18	21	19	20	22	23	24	
25	26	29	27	28	30	31	32	
33	34	37	35	36	38	39	40	
								Total
A	B	C	D	E	F	G	H	

total number of circles in each vertical column and place the number in the total box.

■ PINPOINT YOUR STARTING PLACE ■

The scores in each column indicate the Leverage Points that may benefit you the fastest. While the next chapters are in sequence, they may not be laid out in the order that may most matter for *you*, today. While it makes perfect sense to us to focus on the Leverage Points in order, it may make sense for you to start with a later chapter first. For example, many clients who come to coaching immediately benefit from eliminating the tolerations in their lives. Their physical environment (car, office, house, relationships) is such a mess that they will not be able to focus on the long term until they clean off their desk, literally.

Other clients come to coaching feeling fairly organized but need to gain clarity on what they are really trying to achieve in life. You can start with the big picture and work your way inward toward the day-to-day detail or the other way around. It depends entirely on where you are going to get nice traction right off the bat. Get yourself an early win that will inspire you to go on with your coaching journey—go to the Leverage Point that will help you to do that.

Start with the area where you circled the most numbers. If you have a tie, or a three-way tie, then read and work those chapters in order. If you have so few circled that you can't tell where to start, congratulations! You should concentrate on the two questions that you wrote on page 33. Locate their numbers in the grid, and the column letter will tell you what chapter to go to.

A = CHAPTER THREE: THREE PERSPECTIVES

If you are having challenges understanding the impact you have on people and how you are perceived, this chapter will ask you the right questions. You will learn how to pay more attention to the normal things in your environment that you may now take for granted.

B = CHAPTER FOUR: MASTER YOUR UNIVERSE

This chapter will help you to get clear about what you are trying to achieve, where you will achieve it, and how important other people are to your success.

C = CHAPTER FIVE: MANAGE YOUR GIFTS

You may be thinking it is too late to acknowledge what makes you exceptional. It isn't.

D = CHAPTER SIX: GET YOUR NEEDS MET

It's time to let yourself off the hook for being a superhero. You are only human, and you can use this chapter to figure out how to better accept that disappointing reality.

E = CHAPTER SEVEN: CHERISH AND PROTECT YOUR VALUABLES

You may have ignored what is most vital to you for way too long. It's time to recognize and seek out what will bring you closer to what matters most to you.

F = CHAPTER EIGHT: NAME AND CLAIM YOUR STANDARDS

You know what you think is important. Now it is time to take a stand for it and get your own set of rules. With a defined code of conduct for yourself, your decisions and choices come much more easily.

G = CHAPTER NINE: DRAW AND DEFEND YOUR BOUNDARIES

No one will ever run roughshod over or take advantage of you again, because you will know how to put an end to it. What a relief.

H = CHAPTER TEN: ELIMINATE YOUR TOLERATIONS

You may be putting up with way too much basic stuff. Take care of some of the details. It will feel great and energize you to focus on what's really important.

If you are in doubt, either begin at the beginning and move forward, or start at the end and skip around. Trust yourself to know, and just get started.

CHAPTER THREE

Three Perspectives

. . . and one really good question

How do you see yourself?
How do others see you?
How do you want to be seen?
Now what?

The Three Perspectives are questions that individually lead to useful insights and together provide a 360-degree view of you in your environment. They provide a frame of reference for all the conversations you have with yourself about how you are getting on in the world. They provide a way to logically gain some perspective.

When you begin work with the Three Perspectives, the first thing you'll tackle is working from the *inside out*—How do I see myself? With this question, you examine and get rid of the dysfunctional baggage of old views or versions of yourself that remain superimposed on who you are today. Next you'll work from an *outside in* perspective—How do others see me? We give you the tools you need to get accurate data for answering this question, including feedback from those others.

Once you have some clarity on the first two questions, we'll move into some more complex territory—How do I want to be seen? With this question, all the misguided behavior you engage in ("Who, me?") that causes you to ask "Why did I *do* that?" will become clear. The amount of time-wasting and ineffective behavior uncovered by this question is staggering. With all the time and energy that is freed up by eliminating such behavior, you can then turn to a question of *choice* and *action: now what?*

Snapshot:

Frank is the senior VP of sales for a large, profitable business unit of a media company where he has worked for fifteen years. Five years ago, the company merged with another, larger media company, and he has been navigating the cultural differences ever since. Nothing makes Frank happier than seeing his people win. He's the kind of guy who puts up posters about determination and persistence because he really believes them. Frank is proud of what he has accomplished: his title, his salary and stock options, his seventeen-year marriage. When Frank walks the halls, his presence is announced by the wave of sheer energy that precedes him. He is rarely seen sitting in a chair; he always seems ready to spring. But suddenly he was struggling with how to jump the chasm between the senior management of a business unit and the company's executive group. In his perception, the executive group was a shark tank filled with political masters.

Frank prided himself on his view of himself, and his response to the question How do you see yourself? showed that he saw himself as a "good, solid midwestern boy" who was honest, straightforward, and guileless, not as someone who could succeed in this more complex and dangerous environment. However, with the question How do others see you? Frank learned that those who reported to him saw him differently. They viewed him as their savior—someone who had managed his superiors so skillfully that it paved the way for his unit's tremendous success. His employees also saw him as tough, sharp, and capable of leading the company at the highest level. Learning this was a considerable eye-opener, and Frank began to expand his view of himself.

Now he needed to ask himself the question How do I want to be seen? Was this an obstacle to reaching his goal of making a greater impact on the company? He reviewed how he was seeing himself and how attached he was to having others see him the same way. He looked at how he was going to have to alter this in order to show up as a true leader at the top levels.

There was only one problem, but it was substantial. He couldn't find anyone in the upper management group who fit his idea of what a leader was supposed to be. The closer Frank got to the upper echelon of management, the more he felt that he was barking up the wrong tree. No matter how hard he tried, he just couldn't seem to fit in.

In the end, Frank changed his goal. He could not find a way to be who he needed to be and still be accepted at the company's top level. He was simply too attached to being seen by others the way he saw himself. So Frank switched his sights from being a big shot to being the best leader he could be to the people who were currently working for him. In the meantime he searched for a company with senior leadership he did respect. Frank is now VP of worldwide sales for a rival company, and though he misses his old crew, he knows that he ended up in the right place.

Frank's in-depth examination of the Three Perspectives proved to be an invaluable tool for figuring out how he needed to think in order to get where he wanted to go. He was able to assess his choices and choose to move forward in a way that suited who he was rather than try to bend himself into someone he wasn't and couldn't be.

The Three Perspectives provide us with an opportunity to make choices that are consistent with what we are trying to achieve in life, personally and professionally. We invite you to dig into the Three Perspectives in this chapter, to take a look at yourself with fresh eyes. You may not like everything you see, but we are certain this work will enable you to immediately improve your effectiveness in all areas of your life.

Snapshot:

Simon sits at the conference table with his head hanging down. Actually he is trying to keep his head from blowing off. He knows that it's not physically possible for his head to blow off, but that doesn't keep him from feeling like it just might happen anyway. His hands are clasped together behind his neck, so that it looks as if he is literally hanging on to his head. Simon is smart—his girlfriend laughingly says "too smart to live," and sometimes he thinks this is actually true. His high IQ combined with his prickly personality have painted him into a corner in every single job he's ever had. He is always right and universally loathed for it in the workplace. It is exhausting him.

Colleagues—his team and the client's team—surround him. All eyes are on him. He knows that the decision they made is stupid and wrong and in exactly nine months someone will get fired for it. If it isn't him, he will have the same unbelievably frustrated feeling of "I told you so," and even if he can't resist the temptation to say it out loud, everyone will know that is what he is thinking and despise him anyway.

As Simon lowers his hands, raises his head, and begins to speak, he knows that what he is doing will only hurt him. In fact, he can feel a part of himself watching the scene from a corner of the ceiling. That part of himself is shaking his head and mouthing "You're shooting yourself in the foot, Simon." Despite full knowledge that he should stay silent, Simon feels his mouth open. He pours out the truth as he sees it, a stream of *invectives at the injustice and inefficiency of the systems and the incompetence of several individuals. He can feel the faces around him hardening and the deal slide south as he speaks.*

Impulse control, anyone? he thinks. I have got to find a way to never do this again.

Simon was right, but at what cost?

Simon did have the capacity to choose actions that could help him achieve his ultimate goal. Simon could choose how he was going to behave. However, right now he was simply giving in to his need to be right.

Simon is a good example of how we act out our lives each and every day. We try to engage in the most effective actions that give us the greatest yield for our efforts. We want to create the most effective and rewarding relationships with others with the least amount of drama, stress, and hassle. To achieve this we would do well to approach our lives the way effective actors and leaders do. The approach is: we are always on stage. The judgments and reactions that others make are real and important to our success. Effective actions and ways of being in the world are influenced and driven by the Three Perspectives:

1. How we see ourselves—our self-image and our intention
2. How others see or perceive us
3. How we want to be seen, or how we want to show up in the world (unconsciously and consciously)

We are ultimately responsible for designing the way we live our lives and the results we achieve.

The Three Perspectives help us to thoroughly understand how to deal with the world—and then help us move to create what we want.

Good coaching employs useful concepts from behavioral psychology, anthropology, management and leadership development, philosophy, and the arts. Madeleine's background in classical theater brought her a potentially useful point of view. Actors build their characters in two different ways: from the outside in or from the inside out. Some actors work best by going outside-in: starting with the costume, physical characteristics, and voice of the character and moving inward one layer at a time until they feel the soul of the character they have created. Other actors start from the essence of the character, embracing and connecting with their struggle and passion first and then adding layers until they create the character's external form. Either way, the development of character is about making clear decisions and choices about who you are and what you want to accomplish.

Do as the greats do: commit yourself to that character; make extremely specific choices and then commit to them fully. Actors have the unique opportunity to rehearse their choices and make changes if they do not "read"—which means that people do not "get" what they are attempting to portray. Actors can work themselves sick, but if no one understands what they are attempting to convey, it doesn't work.

As leaders or team members, it is also important that we understand our audience and gain the reaction we intend. Far too often people are unable to create the desired reaction from the important people in their lives. Being able to read others and to use that information to build strong relationships is crucial. If bosses are unable to create effective relationships with their direct reports, they won't have the focus and support required to succeed as a department, team, or business unit. Research by Marcus Buckingham and Curt Coffman in *First, Break All the Rules* clearly shows that the number one indicator of job satisfaction is the quality of the relationship between an employee and his or her manager. When employees have a poor relationship with their manager, how committed do you think they will be to helping the manager succeed?

No one *attempts* to create bad or less than satisfying relationships. No one gets out of bed, looks in the mirror, and says, "I am going to be a big jerk today." Most of us are simply unaware of the effect we have on others. We also do not realize how crucial creating powerful relationships in all aspects of our lives is to our success. Creating effective relationships and accomplishing things with others can be easy, as long as a careful approach is employed. The Three Perspectives offer a simple and straightforward framework to understand who you are, how others see you, what drives you, and finally, what you can do about it.

Now let's take a look at each of the Three Perspectives a little more closely.

Perspective 1: **How do you see yourself?**

Since it is up to each and every one of us to live our own lives, it is important to first get a sense of why you like yourself, what you like about yourself, and what you do not like—who you are from the inside out. This is important because your opinion of yourself is a crucial piece of your personal operating system. Your opinion of yourself needs to be a fine-tuned balance of reflected reality and inventiveness. Because no matter what you accomplish, who your friends and family are, how fast or how smart or how beautiful or how nice you are, if you do not have a healthy image of yourself, nothing else matters.

Dr. Jennifer James, a cultural anthropologist, is an expert on self-esteem and its effects on our societies and social structures. In her research she has studied hundreds of cultures ranging from urban societies to indigenous cultures that are still in relative isolation. She has found that across all cultures self-esteem is affected by four factors:

1. Fate
2. Early experience with adults
3. Life experience
4. Our opinion of each of the above

First, our self-esteem is influenced by fate. Are we born American, English, Japanese, Chilean, Ethiopian, Canadian, Russian, Iranian? And what type of family are we born into? Fate determines the type of life we live.

Second, our early experiences with adults affect our self-esteem. Were we raised in a nurturing family or by people who did not care for us? What type of parents did we have, what type of family? Are we first-born, the second, or a middle child? Were we part of a small or a large family? Whether or not adults paid attention and generally responded positively to us play a large role in our self-image and self-esteem later in life.

Third, life experiences influence self-esteem. War, peace, prosperity, poverty, education, good and bad health, all affect our self-esteem. The experiences we have in life shape us and make us who we are, and more importantly, they shape how we feel about ourselves.

Fourth, our opinion of the above influences shapes our self-esteem. How do we interpret the story of our life? How do we interpret the successes and failures we have had? How do we interpret our family and heritage? Are we proud of where we come from or ashamed? What is our opinion of our family and how it has influenced us? For example, are you proud of what you have accomplished despite your terrible childhood, or does your childhood still haunt you? Are you ashamed you grew up with privilege and money, and do you feel guilty about it? Do you see yourself as a disappointment to your family given all the opportunity you had growing up? Do you feel proud of where you have come from? Do you feel like a hero and an example to your old neighborhood, or do you feel you have "sold out" by leaving your home and your people for a better life? By far the most important aspect of self-esteem is the opinion you have created in your own mind about your life. Are you your own best friend or your own worst critic and enemy?

What is amazing about Dr. James's work on self-esteem is how predictive self-esteem is of success and fulfillment in life.

Consider the following. About ten years ago a story emerged about two brothers who had taken opposite paths in life. One brother was awarded the Nobel Prize for scientific achievement, while the other brother was a convicted ax murderer. The story was widely covered, and it turned out that both brothers had endured a terrible and abusive childhood. This seemed to make the story even more remarkable, that one brother had turned into a murderous criminal and the other a Nobel laureate. Both brothers were interviewed and asked the same question: how did you end up where you are in life, given your abusive childhood? Ironically, both brothers responded to the question identically: "Given my abusive childhood, how could I have become anything else?"

Both brothers were handed the same initial fate, they were raised in the same household. We can also assume that they had similar experiences with their parents early in life, although each brother may have been affected differently. What is remarkable in this story is that the brothers decided to live their lives so differently, despite almost identical early childhood experiences. While life's experiences may affect us greatly, the strongest effect on us as human beings is the perceptions and beliefs we have about the things that occur in our lives.

So what is the story of your life? What fate were you born into? How do you describe your early experiences with adults and with your family? What kinds of experiences have you endured? What experiences have you been blessed with? Answering these questions can help you understand the foundation of your self-esteem. Answer the following questions: what is your opinion of your life's journey up to today? How do you feel about your life? What are you proud of?

The first Perspective provides us with an understanding of how we see ourselves, how we feel about ourselves, and what we like and do not like about ourselves. Understanding how we see ourselves is the first powerful step to getting the most out of life!

Perspective 2: **How do others see you?**

No man—or woman—is an island. We live our lives in relation to others—at work, at home, in our communities. Everyone has at least one relationship that is troubling him or her. The second Perspective can provide you with valuable insights into the way you come across to others. And remember, just because something does not feel good right away does not mean it is not good for you.

 ## Snapshot:

Don is tall and lanky with sharp black eyes that miss absolutely nothing. He pulls into the parking lot on a cool autumn day in his snappy black sports car. The receptionist feels the change in the air as he comes through the door. Don is a star. At thirty-seven he is director of strategic alliance at a top-performing wireless company. He hits the phone at 7:00 A.M., on the way to work, leaving the top up on his convertible so the noise does not drown out the cell phone. He saves the deliciousness of having the top down for the drive home, when it doesn't matter how his hair looks anymore.

He has a reputation for being determined, his senior management team respects him, and he knows they have come to depend on him. Don is in the very rare position of being utterly sure of his own job security. So what's the problem?

Don's employees are terrified of him.

As a result of a 360-degree feedback process and a review by senior management, it has become apparent that although Don excels at getting things done, he does not seem to care about building his team or developing his people. He is not the kind of leadership role model senior management wants to present to the company as an ideal leader.

Enter the coach: Don is thrilled to be singled out for development and has a great, open attitude. He is also a little confused: "They want me to get things done, but then they complain about what it takes to make things happen." In his very first session with his coach, they discuss the feedback that he is terrific "upward" but less effective with his peers and even less effective with his direct reports.

"Yeah, isn't that wild?" says Don.

His coach laughs. "Yeah—do you agree that it's true?"

"Oh yeah," says Don, "but I don't really know how this happened. I really like this company, and I really want to do what I have to do to be successful here."

"Okay," says his coach, "so here's a subject for discussion: politics. Talk to me about politics."

"Oh, I don't believe in politics at all," says Don. "I've never been a brown-noser. I shoot straight from the hip—with everyone." Don went on at length about how much he despises yes-people and how he loathes internal politics and goes to great lengths to avoid getting caught in them.

"Okay, let's take a look at what you do upward [meaning with his bosses] that you are not doing across or downward. What actions do you take, or what actions are different?"

"Well—when I'm with people I respect, I listen more and ask a lot of questions."

"And you listen to the answers?" interjects the coach.

"Well, of course," Don goes on. "When I disagree with them, I think about how I'm going to make the argument so I don't make them look bad. I try to make things sound like their idea because there is much more likelihood that they'll buy into it if I do that."

"That implies that you don't actually respect some of your peers or your direct reports, is that accurate?"

There is an intake of breath and a deep silence.

All of sudden Don says in a hushed voice, "Wow. I just saw it. I guess I am much more of a political animal than I like to believe."

More silence. Then: "Wow. That really stings."

Don chose to look at himself with a new perspective and learned something powerful about himself. Prior to a few simple questions, he had seen himself as aggrieved, confused, misunderstood, and maligned. The next thing you know, he discovers how he has created the situation by treating his senior managers one way and his direct reports and peers another. One minute he is Mister I Don't Have a Political Bone in My Body, and the next he sees clearly how he has become masterful at managing upward without even realizing it. It takes only a few short minutes for him to move from one view to another.

Which is true? Which is real? Does that matter? The coaching question that will always be relevant is: is this realization useful, and what are you going to do about it?

In Don's case, seeing himself more clearly—by carefully considering information about how others see him—helps him focus on behaviors that are going to make his employees feel heard and respected. Moving forward, Don will also be much more attuned to his own behaviors and how they affect others.

At the core, the second Perspective, How do others see you? provides us with valuable information about how we affect others in our environment. Do people respect us? Do they want to be around us? Do we add value to people's lives? Are we kind and courteous? Do we connect? Do we care? Do we add to or take away from another's day? Do we help others? Do we inspire? The number one indicator of success in life, and especially in business, is the capacity to build and leverage relationships. The essence of that capacity is the experience others have when they interact with us.

The second Perspective can get tricky because there are so many different people who see us in so many different ways. We all know folks who place way too much weight on what other people think, and that certainly isn't a great way to go either. So what are we talking about here? Simply, reliable information. You don't need to figure out what people think so that you can be all things to all people. But you do need to *understand how people see you so that you can find the best way to be effective with them.* In Don's case, his boss saw him as so effective that he never would have known how Don's direct reports saw him. Don, frankly, would have remained just as clueless. If Don had wanted to stay in his job, never changing, growing, or moving forward, that would have been fine, though someone would have noticed the body count eventually. If we want to change and grow, we have to understand how we are seen.

One of Don's big epiphanies was that the more seniority he got, the less important "managing up" would be. It seems obvious from the outside, but when we are up to our eyeballs in a situation, we may not be able to see what is right in front of our face. Don also realized that every little he thing he did—every eye roll, every frown, every smile, every little exasperated sigh—carried more weight the higher he went in the organization. Don saw himself as just a regular guy trying to get ahead, but what he didn't take into account was that the higher he rose in the organization, the less the people who worked for him saw him as a regular guy.

How others see us is crucial information. This perspective can help you develop "cat whiskers." Do you know what cat whiskers are for? Most unique traits found in animals have a purpose that can be linked to evolutionary development; for example, the long neck of a giraffe allows it monopolize the leaves no other animals can get to.

Cat whiskers are no different. They grow outward from the head to the approximate width of the cat's skull and rib cage so that the cat won't stick its head in places that are too small for its body. The whiskers don't seem to prevent cats from climbing trees that they can't get down from, so our metaphor fails us at this point. What we want for you is the human radar equivalent of whiskers, so you can continually gather information about your environment and not get stuck where you don't belong.

Perspective 3: **How do you want to be seen?**

Human beings possess an extraordinary capacity to fool themselves. It's standard fare for the stand-up comedians on the comedy channel. Who hasn't laughed at a bad toupee or an outfit that is ill advised for a figure? These are the most blatant examples of what happens when a person confuses how they see themselves with how they want others to see them. It is the adult equivalent of the one-year-old who believes that if they hide their eyes, no one will be able to see them. It can be harmless if it involves only petty vanities, but the cost can mount if the gap between how we want to be seen and how we are actually seen gets too big.

This question is deeply connected to the way we get our needs met. We will be focusing on this leverage point exclusively in Chapter Six, but let's briefly take a look at someone who is being driven by something she hasn't named and doesn't understand.

 ## Snapshot:

It is 4:45 P.M. Lorelei, on the Wednesday of her first week as an associate in the acquisition department of a global import and export company, is running toward the boss's office with a report she has just completed. Jack sees her running and delivers a piercing whistle that stops her in her tracks.

"What?" she says, turning to him.

"When is that due? I thought it was end of day today."

"It is. I wanted to get it in early."

"Oh you don't want to do that," says Jack, shaking his head from side to side.

Lorelei is eager to get work in on time—she is used to underpromising and overdelivering—because she wants to get off on the best possible foot with her new boss.

"Why not?" she asks.

"Okay, here's the deal with Jeannine. She is really, really smart and pretty fair. She is good to work for except for one thing. If you give her your report before the end of the day, she will focus on everything that's wrong with it, get it back to you in fifteen minutes, and tell you she wants the fixes made by the end of the day. Then you'll be here until 10 P.M. Workaholic Dragon Lady doesn't like things left undone. We've all figured out that if you want to go home at a reasonable hour, you don't turn your stuff in till she's gone, and you leave it on her desk."

Lorelei looks dubious—she didn't think there would be anything wrong with her report. Her desk was cleaned off, and she was actually ready to wrap up some last-minute calls and go home. She hated to leave things so late.

"You can try it if you like, go ahead. Find out for yourself. I'll leave the good take-out menus on your desk." Jack smiles warmly and walks away.

Jeannine is standing in the open door of the conference room right around the corner stunned and breathless. She hasn't meant to eavesdrop; it never occurred to her that she might hear something about herself, and by the time she realized what was going on, it just seemed too awful to make her presence known.

Jeannine had no idea she was perceived the way Jack has just described her. Her first instinct is to march into his office and confront him about telling tales and poisoning the mind of the new team member, but she knows enough to take a deep breath and think things through instead *of launching into a reaction. So she waits until the coast is clear, walks slowly to her office, grabs her jacket, and goes out for a long and thoughtful walk around the block.*

What on earth have I done? she asks herself. How did I miss that the people who work for me think of me as an absurd perfectionist and have created strategies to get around me? When did I get so fanatical about details? I never used to be this way. Jeannine remembers back to one of her first management jobs, to the time she got feedback that although her team was doing well, the rest of the company saw her as soft on her people and a little lackadaisical about quality. The effect of that feedback had been galvanizing, and here she was, seven years later, suffering from having overreacted on a grand scale. She walks along, sighs deeply, and shakes her head.

I want people to know how much I care, Jeannine thinks. And how hard I work. I want them to respect and admire my work ethic. But I've overdone it, and now I'm the butt of jokes.

J eannine reacted to feedback seven years ago and made a snap decision about how she *didn't* want to be seen without thinking too hard about it. Habits were created. Her need to be respected and admired created an unintended dynamic. Jeannine had never consciously decided to do specific things to be respected. In fact, she wasn't aware that respect was something she needed. *The truth about needs is that they find a way to get met, whether or not we consent.* We can choose to get them met inappropriately or in a way that causes the least amount of disruption. We can also choose to get needs met consciously or unconsciously. Jeannine's behavior was not serving her or her staff. Luckily she was able to change it once she saw the unintended consequences of an old habit created by an unnoticed need.

■ ONE FINAL QUESTION ■

After you have answered the three questions—How do I see my-self? How do others see me? and How do I want to be seen?—there is one final question to ask: so what do I do now?

Coaching is ultimately about action. The Three Perspectives are only useful if they cause you to take new or more effective action to change the situation you are dealing with. The Three Perspectives force you to stop and think about what is going on so you can better understand it. The information you gather will help you make choices that present themselves every day about how you spend your time and how you treat people.

Jeannine called a meeting the next morning.

"Okay, gang, I'm going to keep this short. It has come to my attention that I have developed a reputation for overfocusing on detail, micro-managing presentations, and creating unreasonable expectations of how late people should work."

Her team looked back at her with widening eyes. She could see the wheels whirring in their heads as they wondered who had been responsible for the leak.

"Did I get good information? Is this accurate?" She looked back at them curiously.

Jack—to his credit, thought Jeannine—nodded his head yes.

"Okay here's the deal—I work long hours and expect all of you to work as long as you need to get the job done to the highest standard. But I also realize that my standards might not be reasonable sometimes. We're going to do an experiment. If you want feedback or help with your presen-tations and reports, I'll give it; otherwise you can use your own judgment. If we continue to get rave reviews, we can stick with this way of doing

things, but the first complaint we get, we go back to the old way. Lorelei, you're a little new to be going it alone, so I'd like you to run all of your stuff by Jack, just for the first month or so until you get the hang of how things are done around here. Jack, is that okay with you?"

Jack nodded.

Jeannine called an end to the meeting, and as she walked out she saw Jack shoot Lorelei a mystified look.

Let's take your personal Three Perspectives Tour right now. For those of you with Internet access, you may also find this activity at the www.leverageyourbest.com Web site. In fact, at the Web site only, you will be able to send a 360-degree feedback survey to friends and colleagues so that you can get a sense of how you are perceived.

First select one of the roles you are currently playing in your life (e.g., vice president, supervisor, cochair of a committee, parent of a fifteen-year-old).

Role_____

Perspective 1. **How do I see myself?**

What am I (really) trying to accomplish?

_____

What do I know to be true about myself in this role?

_____

What drives me in this role? What are my motivations?

_____

What qualities, skills, or traits do I possess that will make me successful in this role? _____

What qualities, skills, or traits do I possess that will get in my way?

_____

Perspective 2. **How do others see me?**

Who matters in this situation: (List them.)

_____

Do I know how each of these people sees me (in this role)?

_____

If no, how will I find out how each person sees me?

_____

If yes, do I care how others see me? _____

If yes, is there any point of view about me I disagree with or ignore?

_____

Am I sure how others see me? What evidence do I have?

_____

Do I check in regularly about how others see me? _____

What do I think people say about me when I am not around?

_____

Perspective 3. **How do I want to be seen?**

What do I wish were true about me that I am not sure is true?

_____

What do I wish others would think about me, even though I am not
sure it is true? _____

Are the people who are important to me proud of me? _____

If so, what are they proud of? _____

Is it something I am also proud of? _____

If not, what do I wish they were proud of? _____

How do I consistently disappoint others?

_____

How do some of these inconsistencies get in my way?

_____

The Crucial Question 4: **So what do I do now?**

How is the above information useful in moving me toward my
Prime Objective? _____

What strategies can I employ to make me more effective and influential in this role?

_____

What strategies could I be using that I am not using?

_____

Are these strategies clear and actionable to me?

_____

What is the cost of doing things the same way I have always done
them? _____

How am I being when I am most effective?

_____

How am I being when I am least effective?

_____

Who is most profoundly affected by the way I act?

_____

When things go wrong, who is always around?

_____

What is the risk of attempting a slightly different way of doing
things? _____

What type of help and support do I need to be more effective and influential in this role?

_____

Thank you for completing the Three Perspectives Tour. How was
the experience for you? Were the questions difficult to answer? Were
they new to you? Are there gaps between the answers to the questions? For example, do you see yourself as the ninety-pound weak-

ling and want to be seen as the hero who saves the day? Where is the biggest gap?

When we ask these questions, people often state that the answers change over time. What we are talking about here is character. What is important about the discussion of character and the choices it involves is that we experience a sense of integrity or congruence among the four questions. Very few people see themselves the same way others do; they rarely see themselves as they want to see themselves. We have yet to meet someone who doesn't feel that they could be more effective in some way.

CHAPTER FOUR

Master Your Universe

*Do you really know
your environment?*

We generally assume that we know where we are and what is going on around us. We are generally mistaken. In some instances, a superficial assessment will do, but in the workplace, depending on a surface scan of our surroundings and the mix of individuals in it can be fatal. To succeed in any environment requires in-depth study of how each aspect affects our ability to reach our goal. Every action taken must be carefully reviewed for possible consequences. If the workplace is described as a jungle, the metaphor extends to include the natural laws of power dynamics, ecosystems, and food chains. One sure way to avoid being a victim in the workplace is to pay close attention to the intricate web of relationships and agendas around you. Then you can make choices instead of feeling battered by unexpected storms. Let's meet Anne, a rising star caught unaware.

Snapshot:

"You lack gravitas." The consulting firm's senior partners surround Anne at the big conference table.

Gravitas? thinks Anne, trying to keep a look of contemptuous hilarity off her highly expressive face. The pompous tone of the discussion about whether to bring her on as a partner is sliding rapidly downhill. Anne is pretty sure she's never heard the word gravitas actually used in a sentence before. "What on earth does that mean?" she asks without inflection, while also congratulating herself for not laughing out loud.

"You smile too much," says the CEO, "you laugh too loudly, and you crack too many jokes. We believe this keeps clients from taking you seriously, and we feel that it will keep you from garnering the respect due a partner in this firm."

Anne's desire to laugh dies as she absorbs the implications of the CEO's words. She feels stunned. She had thought that the CEO enjoyed her buoyant sense of humor. She looks at the faces around the table—the managing partner, with whom she has had a few minor run-ins over admistrivia but who seems nice enough; the brilliant top strategy guy, who has always seemed to tolerate her as a necessary evil; Arlene, the VP of the Northeast region and a key rainmaker, who has brought in top banking clients for whom Anne has done some brilliant work. The VP of human resources had to cancel out of the meeting at the last minute, but Anne thought his might have been a sympathetic face in the sea of inscrutable blank masks.

Anne fights a desire to put her face into her hands and groan. She struggles to keep her fear off her face—to be as unreadable as those at the table. Anne has been at the firm for two years and has always wondered whether she was the right fit for the company and its rather stuffy culture. Though she had known the fit was a little off, she hadn't seen this coming at all. Anne feels as though the rug has been yanked out from under her. They had pursued her to join their consulting company because of her talent and expertise with Information Technology Security. She consistently outperforms everyone in the room in terms of experience and creativity in her subject area. And they know it. Her colleagues have always been polite, but she has never been able to shake the feeling that she's a rough and dusty cowboy in a room with a white carpet and fine china. Her salary is absurdly high, but so are her work hours. She is also worried that making partner could cause her to sell her soul to the 24/7—work-till-you-die-of-it devil. But more importantly, she wonders if she can really succeed among these people who are so different from her.

"I think I inspire respect because of how well I serve the client and because I kick butt in my field," she quips.

"That is exactly the kind of thing we mean, Anne. That kind of colloquialism shouldn't be used on such a serious occasion. You are good at your job, Anne, but we feel you are a loose cannon."

Geez Louise, Anne thinks, I'll never make it here.

Anne is clearly out of her element at this firm; at least that's how she sees it today. Fortunately, Anne is getting this straight from her CEO. He has done her a great service in telling her the truth about how she is perceived. We should all be so lucky to have the Second Perspective—How do others see you?—laid out so clearly. Anne is a little staggered by how unaware she has been. But what should Anne do with this newfound information? Should she try to change her behavior? Should she attempt a dramatic makeover, perhaps enroll in some finishing school? Or should she just give in to her initial impulse to bail and look for a new job where people will accept her style? All good questions that are usually asked by people who feel stuck.

How do you know if you are in the right place? How do you know if your frustrations at work are things you can work past or will be insurmountable obstacles? Most of us sense our frustrations and discomfort at work fleetingly. We are so busy doing our job, it can be hard to pay attention to crucial undercurrents that will affect our success. In the hustle and bustle of the average day, who has the time to think about it? The answer is that no one can afford not to. Even when we get clear feedback, we often don't know what to do with it. So we let it fade into the background where it exerts low-level but constant pressure and becomes a toleration, or we do something radical like quit the job. Neither choice is a good one. It is so much easier to keep our attention on problems we understand well and can solve—to simply keep our heads down, do our jobs, and hope for the best. Hope, unfortunately, is rarely a successful option. Action must be taken, but how to decide what it should be? Here is a way to think it through.

■ FIRST ASSESS YOUR ENVIRONMENT ■

If you have any doubts whatsoever about your place in your work environment and the people in it, you must step back and take a broader look at the whole picture. A tiger can survive in some ecosystems but not in others. Context is as important as the individual. The key to success in any given environment is to break down all of its specific aspects and deal with each one in turn. Breaking down the problem into small chunks makes it easier to deal with. This is not as easy as it sounds—some of smartest people we know struggle with it. Even those whose success at work has been built on their analytical thinking abilities find themselves at sea when it comes to applying the same skills to analyzing their place in their surroundings and how others affect it.

The following series of questions is designed to help you to scan your environment carefully; then you can make choices and pinpoint the areas that will require some thoughtful strategic actions.

The Workplace Scrubdown

Product or Service

Do you believe in/support the product that your company sells?　　　　　　　T　　F

Do you see yourself as being part of something that contributes to the world?　　T　　F

Quality of Clients or Customers

Do you enjoy the people you serve?　　　　　　　　　　　　　　　　　　　T　　F

Do they recognize and appreciate you?　　　　　　　　　　　　　　　　　T　　F

Leadership: Vision, Strategy, Credibility

Do you feel confident that the company's top leadership has the direction and
　growth in hand?　　　　　　　　　　　　　　　　　　　　　　　　　T　　F

Are their actions consistent with their words?　　　　　　　　　　　　　T　　F

Direct Supervisor: Trust, Direction, Support

Does your supervisor make sure you have the resources you need to do your job well?　T　　F

Do you feel that your supervisor is fair?　　　　　　　　　　　　　　　T　　F

Are you expected to put in too much time at work?　　　　　　　　　　　T　　F

Peers: Quality, Competition, Support

Do you feel on a par with the people you work with?　　　　　　　　　　T　　F

Is there enough competition to challenge you?　　　　　　　　　　　　T　　F

Is there enough friendliness to make you look forward to seeing people at the office?　T　　F

Physical Environment

Do you have enough space, light, tools/equipment to get your job done?　　T　　F

If you travel, do you have your systems in place to make it smooth for yourself?　T　　F

Opportunities for Job Advancement or Career Growth

Do you have the opportunity to learn new things and grow? (Only relevant if
　this is important to you.)　　　　　　　　　　　　　　　　　　　　　T　　F

Can you see a career path that will keep you engaged?　　　　　　　　T　　F

Will you be able to achieve your Prime Objective from where you are currently?　T　　F

What evidence do you have that the time and energy invested so far will pay off?　T　　F

Are you compensated fairly according to market value and the state of the economy?　T　　F

If you are currently dissatisfied with your compensation, do you have a clear idea
　of what it would take to increase it?　　　　　　　　　　　　　　　　T　　F

Almost any one of the questions you answered no to will require you to have a serious conversation with your manager. You will need to develop a plan to fix each item over time. The good news, as you will see in Chapter Ten, Eliminate Your Tolerations, is that once you have clearly identified the problems they are much more likely to get solved. The only area that is almost impossible to affect and change is poor leadership—unless, of course, you happen to be on the leadership team, in which case you have your work cut out for you. If you answered no to over half the questions, you might consider looking for a different line of work or work in a different company. If that is the case, you will still require the help of others—people in your industry, headhunters, career specialists, your friends and family. In all cases the thought process is the same, only the roles and names of the players change.

After Anne had recovered from the emotional blow of the meeting, she sat down to think things through. She realized that only one aspect of the job was a real problem. Whatever reservations she had about her work hours, she knew that it wouldn't be different at any other company she wanted to work at. Everything else was good— she had great associates to work with, she really enjoyed her clients, her office was fine, and her assistant was fantastic. It seemed a shame to walk away over one thing. Anne thought about who might be available to work with her.

■ IDENTIFY THE PLAYERS ■

Once you understand the aspects of your work environment that are less than ideal, the next step is to understand how each individual in your vicinity might either help or hinder your efforts to improve things.

People will put up with almost anything if they are surrounded with people they get along with. This is simply a given. But what about all the other ones? The importance of "getting along well with others"—including people of very different personality types, very dissimilar worldviews, or conflicting agendas—has been the focus of a great deal of research in recent years. Research conducted at Bell Labs determined that the number one indicator of success for their leaders was the capacity to build and leverage networks of personal relationships. We have also found this to be true. *The key to your success in achieving your Prime Objective is how well you relate to the people in your life.* What is astonishing is that even when people know this, they ignore it. They hope that if they are competent enough in their work they will be able to get away with not playing nice in the sandbox. Again, hope is an ineffective choice.

Ask yourself about the current state of each of your work relationships. Make a list of all the people you work with and consider how likely they are to lend you a hand with something you might be trying to accomplish. Use the chart on the next page to do this. You might say that it depends entirely on what you ask for, so assume that it is something that affects them and could possibly make them look good (or bad).

List People	Items to Get Help With	How Likely Are They to Help You? On a scale of 1-10 1 = Never in a million years 10 = Trusty sidekick who would do anything for you
Boss(es)		
Subordinates		
Peers/Colleagues		
Customers		

Which of these people will contribute to your plan, even in tiny ways? Who will detract from it?

One clear pattern we see repeated over and over is that people put together a well-researched plan to reach a goal that they intend to carry out *all by themselves*. These are destined to fail. Unless you see yourself as Robinson Crusoe (and even he had Friday), you should figure on needing the assistance and supporting networks of the people around you. No one does it alone; the farther you go, the more you will depend on others. This is simply a fact. One colleague in our industry once said that if leaders could figure out how to get to the end goal by themselves, they would go there and send a postcard. Very true, very funny, and it hasn't happened yet.

What is important to understand about relationships? The research and literature on the subject is vast. While we are not relationship experts, we have gleaned and distilled a few crucial truths. Maybe these are truths you already know but have forgotten. Maybe they're just truths you'd like to ignore. To build and maintain a rock-solid network of relationships that will help you, you must:

Identify what is in it for the other person to help you

Understand what the other person has to lose

Recognize the beliefs, personality type, and thinking style of the other person

Genuinely care about them and show it

No one will help you unless they can see what's in it for them. There, we said it. And like it or not, it's true. If you can absorb this as reality without judging it, you'll be in great shape. Many have a belief that to accept this truth makes them cynical, or worse—manipulative. Only the actions you choose to take based on this truth can be cynical—understanding and using it wisely is simply smart. To reject the reality is to put yourself in the position of being used by those who haven't. We are not trying to say that every person around you is motivated by selfish gain, only that everyone is motivated by something specific and that you have to understand what that is. What does this mean to you? It means you need to look at people from all angles.

■ WHAT'S IN IT FOR ME? ■

Uncover the currency—get clear and specific about what is important to people and why. What *is* in it for the people helping you, and how will you contribute to helping them achieve their aims? Very few people in your life are naturally equipped to help you achieve your Prime Objective. In fact, many people could prevent you from achieving what you truly desire. Not that people have conscious thoughts about derailing your efforts; that would make things much clearer. It is just that most people are so focused on getting through their own lives, they have little time or energy left to help you achieve what you're after in yours.

Begin today to seek to understand the needs, valuables, and aims of your coworkers. As you work through this book and understand better how to leverage what you have going that works, you will also be able to identify the same in others. Where are they trying to go themselves, and what sort of help are they needing along the way? Everyone has an agenda, an approach or an angle they are working, consciously conceived or not. We find that the people who are most effective in building and leveraging relationships understand others profoundly, often better than they understand themselves. Once you get a take on what is driving someone else, it is often easy to help them and, by so doing, *help them help you* along the way. And here's the hard part: you must help them without the expectation of receiving anything in return.

Actually understanding other people and helping them move along their path is one of the most powerful things you can do to get the help you need. The only thing that keeps us from seeing this hard truth is the false notion that if people really loved us, they would help us in the way we want to be helped. Perhaps that is the way things *should* be, but it is not the way things *are*. We have seen people take this to heart, and we have to ask them to snap out of it, get real, and move on. Ask yourself:

What is their *Prime Objective?*
What do they need to achieve it?
What is valuable to them?
What is their secret vanity?

We all have secret vanities: little things we are secretly proud of and hope people will notice. Examples of secret vanities we have sleuthed out include precision and accuracy in work, the neatest office on the floor, a beautiful look and feel to every document produced, the ability to make the team laugh; a keen memory for what was said in an informal meeting.

Why are they secret? This relates to the Third Perspective—How do you want to be seen? They remain secret because we are embarrassed to be so frail, they make us worry that we are vain, or the people we love will not approve of them. Who really knows? It doesn't matter—what matters is that you pay attention to them and respect them. It never serves us to mock or ignore someone's secret vanity.

▪ WHAT IS AT STAKE? ▪

Make it your business to discover what people have to gain or lose if you are successful. Believe it or not, your friends and family do not always have your best interests at heart, especially when you are trying to create a better or more fulfilling life for yourself. We call this "small town inertia," but it happens in all environments. When people know you and love you as you are, it causes extreme discomfort when you change. Why? One of two reasons. The first is the simpler one: people who care about you fear that they will lose you if you are successful. The other is more complex: people will compare themselves to you and find themselves wanting. When you come from the same environment and you pull ahead of the pack, all people can think about is what your success says about them. Why aren't they as successful? This phenomenon occurs in many cultures. In Australia they call it the "tall poppy syndrome," in Japan they call it the "tall nail." The tall poppy gets its head cut off—the nail gets pounded down. The idea is that if you stick out in any way, you'll draw negative attention. In the United States we'd like to pretend this isn't so, but the phenomenon exists all the same. We say "the squeaky wheel gets the grease" here, but that doesn't change the fact that people hate the squeaking.

Fundamentally, people hate change. If you are shaking things up for yourself, it *will* cause change for others, whether you intend it or not. You must recognize this though you might not know what to do about it. One thing to do is to simply talk about it. You can assist people around you in managing the change you are creating by helping them to understand how it will affect them personally and how it will affect your relationship. Let them know what they can expect in the future, how you see them fitting into your life. Let them know that you have thought about them and that they matter to you. Another thing to do—and this can be extremely painful—*is to let go of relationships with people who insist that you stay the same so that they can remain comfortable.* Chapter Nine, Draw and Defend Your Boundaries, will offer you a great deal of help in this area.

■ RECOGNIZE DIFFERENCES ■

It is crucial in mapping relationships that you understand in detail the ways in which others are different from you. Just because something is self-evident to you does not mean it is obvious to others. It is key to consider how others around you absorb information and make decisions. They may be extremely visual and require something to be literally spelled out on a flip chart. Or they may want to hear the whole story in detail with repetition. Or they may prefer to have it in writing and have time to think about it.

These distinctions can be difficult to identify, but people will give you clues. Notice when someone uses "I see" when they understand something versus "I hear you." Those are clues as to whether they are visual and need to see things, or auditory and prefer to hear them. Notice if people ask for e-mails rather than voice mails. People who ask for more detail than you've given will probably always want all the data—others will ask you to cut to the chase and get to the point. You have to be ready for both. Watch for the eyes glazing over—you have given either too little or too much data, but either way you've lost them. Little tidbits of information that you pick up will help you to communicate more quickly with the people who matter to you. *People are much more inclined to be helpful if you make an effort to get on their wavelength.*

■ SHOW REGARD ■

G et interested in people for their own sake, not because you want something from them. This is a paradox. The more interested you become in others without expecting something in return, the more they will be interested in helping you. Listen to people, find a way to care about them, and get interested. Before you know it, people are reaching out to help you right and left. We all know people who try to show that they are interested, but it's clear that their actions are phony. How can you be interested and caring without being phony? Simple: be genuinely curious about people. Try to learn something new about them every time you meet. Listen to them intently, and let them finish expressing their thoughts. Ask them about themselves. Volunteer information about yourself that seems aligned with what they have offered about themselves. Stop talking when you see their eyes glaze over—which means you have to pay attention to others while you are talking. Listen more than you talk. Listen more than is comfortable. Listen more than you already do.

Let's take a look at how this might apply to Anne's situation. When Anne took a moment to map out the key relationships in the partner decision, she made a list of the key players, noting what they had to gain and lose, their main differences in style, and how much of a relationship she had managed to build with each one. It looked like this:

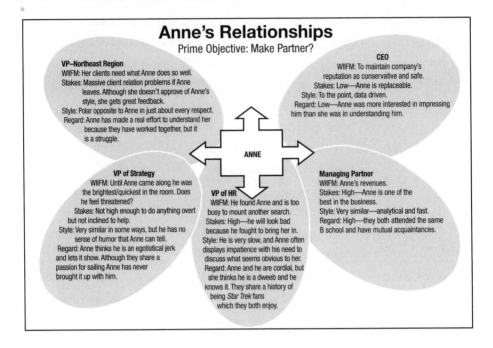

Anne's Relationships
Prime Objective: Make Partner?

VP—Northeast Region
WIIFM: Her clients need what Anne does so well.
Stakes: Massive client relation problems if Anne leaves. Although she doesn't approve of Anne's style, she gets great feedback.
Style: Polar opposite to Anne in just about every respect.
Regard: Anne has made a real effort to understand her because they have worked together, but it is a struggle.

CEO
WIIFM: To maintain company's reputation as conservative and safe.
Stakes: Low—Anne is replaceable.
Style: To the point, data driven.
Regard: Low—Anne was more interested in impressing him than she was in understanding him.

ANNE

VP of Strategy
WIIFM: Until Anne came along he was the brightest/quickest in the room. Does he feel threatened?
Stakes: Not high enough to do anything overt but not inclined to help.
Style: Very similar in some ways, but he has no sense of humor that Anne can tell.
Regard: Anne thinks he is an egotistical jerk and lets it show. Although they share a passion for sailing Anne has never brought it up with him.

VP of HR
WIIFM: He found Anne and is too busy to mount another search.
Stakes: High—he will look bad because he fought to bring her in.
Style: He is very slow, and Anne often displays impatience with his need to discuss what seems obvious to her.
Regard: Anne and he are cordial, but she thinks he is a dweeb and he knows it. They share a history of being *Star Trek* fans which they both enjoy.

Managing Partner
WIIFM: Anne's revenues.
Stakes: High—Anne is one of the best in the business.
Style: Very similar—analytical and fast.
Regard: High—they both attended the same B school and have mutual acquaintances.

Anne examined her Prime Objective: she had entered her MBA program and toughed out her first three jobs expressly because she was aiming for the top, the best, the crème de la crème: the consulting firm that made the top three of *Fortune*'s "50 Most Desirable MBA Employers" list every year running. She knew that if she made it there, she could write her own ticket. Anne had a plan and she had worked it; now she'd hit a glitch. Anne realized that she would have to construct a campaign to counterbalance the impression she had made and rebuild some relationships. She made herself a "to-do" list:

⟶ Clients respond well to me—find a way share that data with the CEO and find a way to assuage his fear that I am harming his desire to maintain the image of the company.

⟶ Get VPs of Northeast and HR to help me collect the data about feedback from clients.

➡ Brainstorm with colleagues about how that might be done.

➡ Book one-to-one meeting with managing partner to get advice about behavior changes and get clear insight into what would turn around perception.

➡ Book lunch with VP of strategy, build relationship with him, and ask him for help.

➡ Call business professor and mentor for some tips—he seems a lot like me and has worked for decades in stodgy environments.

One of the things that shocks Anne is how time-consuming all these activities are going to be. She worries that since she isn't really all that sure of what she is doing, it could be a waste. She decides to take a couple of actions and see where they lead. She also worries that the VP of strategy sees her as a threat, has the ear of the CEO, and could be working against her. Anne hates politics and has always seen engaging in political activity as beneath her. She figures that she'll try to get him to go to lunch and get to the bottom of his reaction to her. She isn't sure she'll be able to disguise her aversion to him, but she plans to spend the meeting trying to understand what matters most to him and why.

▪ PERSONAL POWER AND POLITICS ▪

Those who complain that they don't have the power to achieve their aims are forgetting this simple rule: holding a certain position will give you power, but it is temporary unless you also have personal power. Personal power is defined as the strength that comes of making and maintaining sincere and deep interpersonal connections with others.

This point is particularly important in the workplace. Organizations spend millions of dollars to instill values of excellence, initiative, and ownership in their people, but they ignore the fact that it

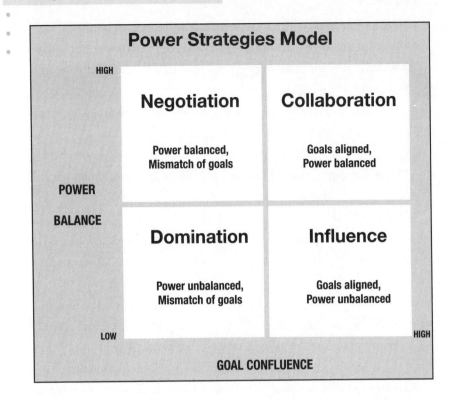

takes enormous courage for people to stick their necks out and shine. Being really, really good at something may be rewarded in the long term but can exert heavy personal cost in the short term. Few have the required political savvy to carry it off. As we try to achieve our goals and objectives, we inevitably call into play political dynamics that are often under the surface and difficult to see. John Eldred, a dear friend and a wonderful teacher and consultant from the Wharton School, University of Pennsylvania, developed a model that illustrates these political dynamics. John's Power Strategies Model has helped countless clients understand what might be happening under the surface in their workplace.

Power balance describes the degree to which each person in a particular pair or group possesses either positional or personal power. When power balance is high, power is shared or is relatively equal; when power balance is low, one person has significantly more power than the other. Goal confluence measures the degree to which each of your individual goals is in alignment or compatible with those of another.

When *power balance and goal confluence are high,* a dynamic of cooperation is created and relationships are naturally easy to develop and maintain.

When *power balance is high but goal confluence is low,* meaning that there is equal footing but each foot is going in a different direction, a condition is created where we can negotiate.

When *goal confluence is high and power balance is low,* power is irrelevant because both parties are going in the same direction. This creates a condition in which both people can influence each other.

The most dangerous quadrant is where *power balance and goal confluence are both low.* When this occurs the party without the power feels dominated and oppressed by the other. Oppression and domination are obviously extremely uncomfortable conditions, but more importantly, individuals and groups who are dominated will respond in one of four ways: *submit, submerge, engage in open conflict, or sabotage.* This is important if you feel that any of your employees or colleagues either avoid you (submit/submerge), are actively trying to make you look bad (sabotage), or verbally attack you in meetings (open conflict).

This situation in the workplace is remarkably common; it is a chief source of stress. It can be extremely helpful to examine who is behaving this way and why that might be so. What do you do that is making another person feel dominated by you? It might be something you are not aware of; it might be something you haven't even done yet but that others fear you might do in the future. There is tremendous value to identifying clear goals so that there are no mistakes about goal confluence. It is also crucial to understand that if you choose to exert positional power without a fair amount of buy-in from others you will come up against intense resistance. Finally, it is important to know that even if you don't have positional power but are clearly rising in the organization due to your talent/hard work, others might feel dominated regardless of your position.

Let's take a look at how these ideas are helpful to Anne in her situation with the VP of strategy. When she thinks about what his goals are, she realizes that she has never asked him and doesn't know. Hmm. Interesting. Her aim right now is to make VP, become a partner in the firm, and head up the Information Technology Security group, which she knows is only going to grow over the next five years. Since her adversary is already a partner, he has more power than she does, but she sees that it is possible that he fears the day when their positional power may be equal. He hasn't sabotaged her yet, but he could. She wonders if maybe he is aiming for CEO down the line and perhaps fears that she will be competition for him. The thought makes her laugh, but she sees that it could be true. She decides that over lunch she will ask him what his goals are, share her goals, and help him to see the degree to which their goals are compatible—that in fact she could be in a position not to compete with him but to make him look good. Either way she sees how at least trying to build their relationship can't hurt.

Not everyone can or should try to fit into their environment. If it means bending yourself into something that is no longer recognizable, it will not be sustainable. But there is a huge gap between small shifts with new habits and a radical makeover, just as there's a gulf between vague dissatisfaction and "Oh my god, I have to get out of this job." It is just that on some days, they can feel like the same thing. Certainly dissatisfaction in too many areas over time can add up to a burning desire to quit and start over someplace else. Putting up with too much will blot anything good. The problem with that, of course, is that whatever situations you are running into now will simply pop up in your next job. You'll still have to build a powerful network of relationships and build a plan to leverage them well.

To be a master of your universe you must understand your Prime Objective—the tangible end that when attained will leave you proud and satisfied. You must understand how to create a viable plan to achieve your Prime Objective with an emphasis on getting into action as quickly as possible so that your experiences and learning will help you achieve your ends. The final and most critical aspect of mastering your universe is understanding how the people in your life and the dynamics of your relationships with them contribute to your movement toward your Prime Objective.

- Seek feedback, be grateful when you get it, and never ignore it.
- If you find yourself griping about work, get specific about it, map out the players, and get to work on it.
- Your ability to relate to those around you is the single most important indicator of success in achieving any goal.

CHAPTER FIVE

Manage Your Gifts

▪ ▼ ▪

*What does it cost you to let
your gifts go unacknowledged?*

Every person comes into this world with gifts, god-given talents, skills, and attributes, qualities that make them unique. The gifts we receive are thrust upon us as infants, deep within our DNA. Sometimes we inherit gifts from our parents or families, but just as often we receive gifts that are outliers—that make us different from our families. The law of heredity that governs who gets what gifts can seem mischievous. The best you can do is understand, accept, and maximize the gifts you have been given to the fullest extent you can. We chose the word *manage* very carefully because we know hundreds of adults who continue to struggle with their gifts late into life, unable to leverage them to generate the success they expected or even feel entitled to. Some are unaware of the impact that their gifts have on others. Gifts are a fascinating aspect of human beings because each one carries with it a complex set of responsibilities and sometimes a hidden dark side.

Snapshot:

Harry is thirty-seven years old and widely acknowledged as the company's best manager. Everyone loves Harry, and his team consistently exceeds expectations. When the training and development group brought in a Coaching Skills workshop, Harry was the coaching poster child. Everyone goes to him for advice about employees who are not living up to potential or who are turning into "problem children." Harry has a big open face, and when he speaks, he paints pictures in the air with his large expressive hands. Sometimes people stop outside conference rooms where he is making a point just to watch the show. He is teased mercilessly about his ties with Disney characters on them. All year round he has candy in his office, the really good stuff that people actually want.

His team's success has led to an increase in head count, and while Harry works hard at trying to keep up his excellent one-on-one meeting standards, he is beginning to lose steam.

In a recent meeting, his boss told him that two of his stars were being transferred to flagging departments and that their replacements had much less experience. Harry left the meeting feeling demoralized despite his boss's words: "Harry, you are so good at this, it'll be easy for you." In a subsequent conversation with a colleague, he realized that he felt punished rather than rewarded for his excellence.

His friend Stan laughed and said, "Harry, get a clue! Don't you know that no good deed goes unpunished?"

Harry committed himself to pulling back and saving his own skin.

What is wrong with this picture?

Harry is gifted at leading teams and individuals. He is a great manager, and people not only love to work for him but thrive under his tutelage. However, it does appear that Harry's gifts have ceased being an asset to him personally and are now a liability. Being a gifted manager has created a situation where he feels taken advantage of. He feels used. And in turn, if Harry stops using his gift for the benefit of others or burns out, it will become a liability to his organization. Luckily, however, Harry finds a way to wrestle back control of his gift rather than just taking it on the chin.

Back to Harry:

A couple of days go by while Harry frets. He realizes he needs some help to think this one through and he shoots Stan an e-mail: "Stano. So no good deed goes unpunished, eh? I need you to explain that one to me. How about a beer at the Condor this evening and you can give me a crash course."

Stan's reply is immediate: "See you in the lobby at 6:00 P.M. sharp. And thanks for giving me a good reason to walk out of here at a decent hour for a change."

Stan and Harry are installed in a booth at the back of the local watering hole by 6:07 P.M. Their friendship goes back to business school, and they were amazed at the fluke that brought them both to the same company. Stan's star has risen a little faster than Harry's, due in part to the fast growth of the Finance Department, as well as to the perception that Stan is a mover and shaker. To the less admiring, Stan is seen as a shark.

"Here's the deal, Harry. You are a natural manager. You care, you teach really well, you know when to let people take off and try their wings, you make people feel good about themselves. Your people would take a bullet for you, and nobody can figure out how you do it. What's more, you seem able to teach your people how to do it the way you do it, so they become natural managers too. That's why your people are always going to get pinched as soon as they're ready. You have set yourself up to lose, my boy."

"Fine, Stan, I agree with your assessment, but what am I going to do

about it? It seems unfair that I should be penalized for doing something so well."

"Absolutely, but I'll say to you the same thing I say to my kids, Harry: There's no such thing as fair. There's only what you are willing to take for yourself."

Harry laughs and says, "That's a harsh world you live in, Stan." Yet he knows Stan has a point.

Stan sighs. "You're a nice guy, Harry, and it would be a waste of your talent for you to finish last. So here's the plan: A. Figure out the exact dollar amount that you're saving that fat and happy boss of yours. B. Insist on getting a bonus every time someone gets pinched from you. That way you'll see the upside of what you are doing. Otherwise you're letting yourself be taken for granted, not to mention the fact that your boss is taking advantage of you and always has been. All they talk about around here is how they want us to 'develop our people,' but there's nothing in the performance system to reward it. If anyone can make it happen, Harry, it's you."

"What if he says no?"

Stan lifts his eyebrows, "Come on, get serious. What would your boss do without you? Harry, you're the best, and he knows it; stand up for yourself for crying out loud! If he says no, you threaten to walk. Then go out and dig up some interest just to scare him."

"Okay, now I'm officially freaked out. Let me think about this."

Harry examined how he had allowed his gifts as a people developer to be taken for granted. He devised a plan to point out to management how valuable his particular talents were and demand protection for his team in the future. Now that Harry was clear on the value of his gift to the organization, he would see one of his people being taken from his leadership as a compliment rather than an attack. The shift in perspective Harry made had a side benefit as well; it caused him to enjoy his job even more. Now that Harry fully acknowledged his gift as a great developer of talent, he became even better at it and over the years developed a reputation throughout the firm as the starting point for many of the firm's rising stars. And Harry also received bonuses for this excellence in growing people. What Stan said over a beer was true, his boss could not live without him!

Understanding your gifts is at the heart of coaching. Olympic coaches focus on what's best and on minimizing weakness in their athletes. Leveraging what is already working will radically improve the quality of your life without making you feel like you have to become something you are not. Leveraging your gifts, and managing their downsides, will help you to become even *more* than what you already are.

You may be asking, Why should I be focusing on where I am already strong when I have problem areas that need care and attention? What about my weaknesses that need rounding out? As with Harry, we are all born with a certain number of natural assets and gifts. To be optimally productive and reach our Prime Objective, a key foundational piece is to turn the heat up on what you've got going for you. Learning to leverage your gifts and strengths is smarter and more efficient than wasting time fixing everything you are no good at.

A dear friend and mentor of ours is one of the most prolific attorneys in his field. He is not only accomplished in the courtroom but a regular contributor to the most prestigious law reviews and business journals and a highly sought-after public speaker. The victim of his success, our friend often felt his life was out of control and not as satisfying as he imagined it would be at this stage of his life. On our urging, he hired a coach to see if he could get some answers or some insights to his dilemma. After a year or so with his coach he had taken back control of many aspects of his life, had learned to say no to many opportunities, had gotten his health under control, and was feeling more peaceful and productive than he had felt in his entire life. He and his coach had a conversation after the holidays, at the start of the New Year. During their conversation, our friend said that this year he was committed to being better organized than in years past. His coach asked him a few questions about his desire to be more organized to see if there was something beneath the surface that would come clear. In the conversation, our friend shared that his overflowing desk and ransacked-looking office had always been the subject of ridicule among his colleagues. Further, he had always seen himself as very productive despite his overall lack of discipline and organization. After a few minutes the coach stopped the conversation and said, "Why don't we skip getting organized this year?"

Our friend did not understand. "What do you mean, skip it this year? I've been disorganized for thirty years, and it's time to put an end to it."

The coach then said, "We've been working together for a year, and I think I know you fairly well by now. I have never worked with anyone more productive and able to make the important decisions. And I believe that the way you organize your life and your piles is a part of you that it does not serve you to change in the greater scheme of things. What would it look like to skip this one and shift our discussion toward what else you would like to accomplish this year?"

Our friend was skeptical but decided to move on in the discussion and focus on other things. It took a few days for him to realize what had occurred as a result of the conversation. He realized that he had been judging himself since he was in high school about his organizational skills. There was a little part of himself that felt he was somehow weak and undisciplined because he had a messy office. The conversation with his coach enabled him to let go of this negative judgment about himself and focus on what he was good at, which was just about everything else in his life!

Understanding and focusing on your gifts and minimizing your attention to the things that are not your strengths can help you squeeze the most out of life.

In addition to learning to focus on your gifts and strengths, we also examine some of the potholes people encounter when they work with their gifts. Every gift presents you with an opportunity, but every gift also comes with a potential dark side. Some gifts have enormous dark sides, and if we are unaware of them, they can cause serious problems.

By recognizing the gifts we possess and the value they bring, we can better leverage them for our own good and the good of others. Does this seem obvious to you? Does using your gifts seem like common sense? It certainly does to us, but we continually experience that it is *not* common practice. So many people understand the notion of gifts instantly, and yet when they take an inventory, they realize that they do not leverage their gifts to their fullest and have in fact been struggling with managing their gifts their whole lives. We even meet people who deny their gifts altogether, which is the biggest shame of all.

■ WHY ARE GIFTS SO DIFFICULT ■ TO MANAGE?

Over the past few years a lot of attention has been paid to the value of discovering and leveraging your strengths. In their book *First, Break All the Rules: What the World's Greatest Managers Do Differently*, Marcus Buckingham and Curt Coffman shared their discovery about the key differentiator between the best managers and the mediocre ones. It is their ability to consistently build upon and leverage the strengths of their employees while finding creative ways to downplay the impact of their employees' weaknesses. They found that the best managers broke the time-honored but erroneous idea that we must round out our shortcomings as individuals if we are to be successful. Of all the things that Buckingham and Coffman un-covered in their extensive research, we were most intrigued by the fact that the greatest managers understood the concept of gifts intu-itively. We were also not surprised that understanding and leverag-ing employee's strengths is not a natural tendency of the less than great managers. As obvious as the concept may be, it flies in the face of centuries of cultural dogma that tells us to be well rounded and to overcome our flaws instead of just building upon our gifts.

People do not consciously choose to make poor use of their gifts—that would just be too stupid. People do not manage their gifts well because they misunderstand their gifts in one or more of three ways.

1. **If something comes easily, it can't be that valuable.** Come on, admit it, secretly in your heart you believe this. We hear it all the time, "no pain, no gain." We often deny our gifts not because they are not special but because they came to us so easily. Haven't you ever known a natural athlete, that boy or girl who looked like they were born with a tennis racket in their hand? Or a natural singer, capable of creating awe in their audiences from an early age? Or that gorgeous kid from down the block, so perfect-looking that people stop and stare when they walk down the street? Bearers of gifts such as athleticism and beauty are rarely appreciated for their gifts—just the opposite in fact. People who manifest gifts early in life are often seen as having their gifts handed to them on a silver platter. Even though we know that to take a natural gift and turn it into a refined skill takes a lot of practice, stories about the gifted often focus on their fall from grace rather than their struggle. Remember the cautionary tale of Casey at the Bat, about the best hitter who failed because of his

overconfidence and arrogance. In fact, most of the stories we hear as children are about the little guy who succeeds due to perseverance and tenacity despite being short on natural gifts.

"I think I can, I think I can, I think I can"—we would challenge you to find an American child who hasn't heard the story of The Little Engine That Could. What is easy to miss, of course, is that the ability to persevere in the face of danger or disappointment is as great a gift as any other.

Just because a gift may come easy to you does not mean that it should be discounted. Just because it's natural to you doesn't mean it isn't special. Harry had tremendous gifts: patience, empathy, the ability to teach, thoroughness, and persistence with people, but he was overly humble about them. Coaching and developing others came so naturally to Harry that he undervalued those abilities. He didn't need to work hard to be good at those things, so he didn't think he deserved credit for them. And it was only a matter of time until others did the same. Once Harry identified his gifts, he was able to strategize a way to have them perceived as more meaningful to himself and others. Do you have any gifts you may be undervaluing?

2. **Don't toot your horn.** Have you heard that old song? The second reason people often undervalue their gifts is that many were raised to do exactly that. God forbid that we stand out or be thought of as pretentious or conceited. In some family cultures it is simply considered to be bad manners.

"He thinks pretty highly of himself, doesn't he?"

"She believes her own press."

"Boy, is he full of himself."

Nobody wants people saying these things about them. This is connected to the Third Perspective—How do you want to be seen? We would generally prefer to be seen as humble; humility is so attractive. It's not considered nice or attractive for a person to openly acknowledge how talented he or she is; how courageous, principled, or smart; how intuitive, organized, and inspiring. For a society steeped in the Judeo-Christian tradition that preaches against hiding one's light under a bushel, we are certainly in the dark when it comes to gifts. But covering up a gift to fit in is one thing, leaving it on the shelf to rot is another.

"Who do you think you are?" This phrase captures the essence of homes where gifts were not only undervalued but actually the subject of abuse. In its most destructive context, that question is a put-down, an insidious way to enforce conformity. This biting question is often thrown out as a way to reel us in, keep us in our place, remind us of someone else's idea of who we should be. *"Who do you think you are?"* is a question many of us also associate with school and an early overbearing teacher. With this question we are taught that by acknowledging or speaking of our gifts and abilities we are committing the sin of claiming we are better than others. To many, the sin of pride is so awful that it must be rooted out at all costs.

Underneath the fear of having children who are conceited is a deep, often unconscious fear that conceit is also dangerous. Conceit invites God and the forces of the universe to teach a lesson to those who think too much of themselves. But in many cases the well-intentioned lessons administered by parents and teachers are not received in a balanced way. Rather, these messages are taken so seriously that they impact us too strongly for our own good. Gift? What gift? If you are not in an environment that supports your particular gift, you may not have recognized it as one. The ancient fairy tale of the Ugly Duckling is the perfect example of natural gifts placed in an environment where they are a liability rather than an asset. We have a friend who grew up to the refrain of "Oh quiet down, don't be so dramatic," and she now works as a speaker richly rewarded for the vibrant, charismatic expression that drew all that childhood criticism. In one environment high-spirited volubility is a curse, in another it is an asset.

When a gift is seen as a curse or as something to be rooted out, the habit of denying it is a hard one to break. The most effective people understand and fully accept their assets yet have a healthy perspective on their value. They appreciate and leverage their gifts while remaining humble and thankful for them.

3. **Beware the green-eyed monster**. The final reason we often have trouble with our gifts is that we have experienced them as provoking the wrath of others. From childhood we learn that those who excel in life are often the victims of jealousy and contempt from their peers. Why some have gifts that make them popular and others suffer from the envy of people is a bit of a mystery.

What we do know is that to not expect others to be envious of our gifts is naive. What is the reward for children born with intelligence and the ability to breeze through school? They are often labeled smart aleck or brownnose. This lesson is carried on through high school and into the workplace. Others often loathe people with extraordinary intelligence. And if you combine intelligence with another gift such as physical attractiveness, the critics really take it personally. How many times have we seen smart women dress down to hide their beauty? Why would they do this, especially in a society that places such a premium on attractiveness? Because they have learned along the way that being gifted with beauty actually undermines the perception of their intelligence.

Do any of these reasons resonate with you? Is it possible that you have denied or hidden a valuable gift that is going to waste? Now it's your turn to assess your gifts, all of them, even the ones you may not have owned up to until now.

In the chart below make a list of your gifts. If you aren't sure it is a gift, assume it is. Use the questions in the right-hand column to prompt and guide you in answering the questions in the left-hand column. Write your answers in the left-hand column.

My Gifts Identification Worksheet

I have a gift for:	
1.	What do I naturally, easily, and effortlessly do when no one is looking?
2.	What about me inspires others, even though it is easy for me?
3.	What did I learn easily and continue to develop effortlessly?
4.	What do I get compliments on that I never even have to think about (e.g., humor, perceptiveness, style, logical thinking, physical courage, a flair for design)?
5.	What about me makes people jealous?
6.	What do I know is special about me but try to hide?
7.	What about me gives me guilty pleasure?
	What is my secret vanity?

Now you have a preliminary sense of your gifts—and you are wrestling with what is getting in the way of nurturing and growing them. It is time to consider some principles about gifts that will be useful in helping you to understand them better. Gifts can be double-edged swords because they sometimes carry liabilities. As we reviewed the reasons we deny or hide our gifts, some of the liabilities became clear. All gifts have a potential dark side; these principles should help you to manage that. Not all of these principles will apply to you—they are rules of thumb.

■ RULES OF GIFTS ■

⟹ We can have an unlimited amount.
⟹ We must identify and take responsibility for the impact our gifts have on others.
⟹ Just because we can do something well doesn't mean we should do it.

THE RULE OF UNLIMITED GIFTS

Our culture tells us that we shouldn't have "too much"—too many positive attributes, too much money, love, or opportunity. It is regarded as unseemly and makes others uncomfortable. Envy and covetousness do not bring out the best in people, and the green-eyed monster can cause all kinds of negative attention. For example, a woman can be regarded as either successful or friendly, but people can become suspicious when she is both. Her peers might talk about how much they hate her if she is also generous and kind. Having a gift or a powerful combination of gifts requires great responsibility on the part of the bearer.

As we've said, our families keep us humble as well, partly for reasons covered in the previous section but also to maintain a sense of equity between siblings. We hear it all the time: "My brother is the smart one; I was always the friendly one." But where is it written that you are allowed only one gift? People have a tendency to limit themselves and others in the number of gifts they are allowed to have. This limit is completely artificial. In fact, we have found the opposite to be true. Where there is one gift there are often many. Most people have much more than one gift.

This points to another aspect of this rule: the multiply gifted must choose where to focus. It isn't that common but it is hard to deal with when it does occur. Some people just have more gifts than they can possibly play with all at the same time. The people we have worked with over the years who really require help with managing their gifts are the ones who have way too many. When people have too many gifts, trying to focus on too many things at once can be overwhelming. A person who has multiple powerful gifts is required to make difficult choices about priorities. Remember, the rule is that you can have unlimited gifts. But each gift must be managed individually if you are to avoid the effect of its dark side. Even if you choose to do nothing with a gift, it has consequences, if not from you, then potentially from others.

Marianne Williamson, in her book *A Return to Love,* captures the essence of what we would all like to believe about gifts. The quote has inspired millions—it is a wonderful vision. Nelson Mandela used it in his inauguration speech to great effect.

Our deepest fear is not that we are inadequate. Our deepest fear is that we are powerful beyond measure. It is our light, not our darkness, that most frightens us. We ask ourselves, who am I to be brilliant, gorgeous, talented, fabulous? Actually, who are you not to be? You are a child of God. Your playing small doesn't serve the world. There's nothing enlightened about shrinking so that other people won't feel insecure around you. We are all meant to shine, as children do. We were born to make manifest the glory of God that is within us. It's not just in some of us; it's in everyone. And as we let our own light shine, we unconsciously give other people permission to do the same. As we're liberated from our own fear, our presence automatically liberates others.

We love this vision—and we also know that it is a bit like Martin Luther King's "I have a dream." Humankind is headed in this direction, but we aren't there yet. We believe that our deepest fear *is* that we are powerful beyond measure. But we also recognize that our fear is of the *responsibility* that comes with power; our fear is that others won't use our light as permission but will hold our glory and our power against us. Because that is what people experience all the time. Which brings us to the next rule.

THE RULE OF RESPONSIBILITY FOR IMPACT

The second rule about gifts is that we must identify and take responsibility for the impact our gifts have on others. It takes enormous courage to do this, and we aren't always up to it. When we succeed, we often receive the support and accolades of those around us. Unfortunately, success often comes with a few things we did not plan on. Our success often makes others feel uncomfortable with us and with themselves. For those who see the world in black and white, if someone is winning, it means someone is losing. If you receive a promotion, it can be a great win for you but also a loss for someone else. Fairly or unfairly, you may be judged for your success and resented for it. This dynamic is accepted within families as sibling rivalry, where brothers and sisters experience strong feelings of competitiveness and one-upsmanship. While siblings also love each other and want each other to succeed, they often find themselves competing their entire lives.

Relationships with coworkers, colleagues, and friends can be very similar to sibling rivalry. So as you consider the gifts you possess and how you can best leverage them, remember that with every gift, you must also understand the way your gift or your success may affect another. This is particularly true if you have several worthwhile gifts. Those who see themselves as having few gifts or options might hate you for having so many. This is just a fact of life you have to learn to live with. The only way we know of to deal with these kinds of people is to be unfailingly kind to them. And use their behavior as a reminder to look at yourself and see how you might be doing the same thing in another arena of your life.

Here are some other ways people may respond to your gifts and what you can do about it.

Some people may idealize you and your abilities. When you are idealized, it can create unrealistic expectations for your performance and your conduct. When you turn out to be human, not living up to overly high expectations, you may be blamed or attacked. Pay close attention to people who seem to be overly complimentary or adoring. They can end up being very dangerous if you disappoint them. Be clear about just what you can deliver and be careful never to promise too much. Manage their expectations and agreements scrupulously, remind them of your weaknesses, and let them see you sweat so they don't get the idea that you are breezing by.

Other people may spend a lot of time and effort competing with you instead of focusing on their own growth, development, and performance. It isn't your responsibility to point this out to them, but you can take care not to let yourself get caught in a race you didn't sign up for. When others decide to compete with you it only becomes your problem if they are willing to sabotage you to win. Then you have to confront them and draw a boundary.

Finally, if one of your gifts is charisma or strong personal power, you need to know about a phenomenon that is extremely tricky to diagnose. It isn't that common, but it does happen, and it is downright creepy when it does. This phenomenon occurs when an individual sees you as more powerful than they are, and they give you power over them, in their own minds. They don't tell you about it, so you are not privy to the arrangement. They give you more power than you want or than you asked for and then they resent you for it.

Weird? You bet it is. So here you are with someone who resents you for reasons you cannot fathom.

"What did I ever do to her?" you think. The answer is nothing; you just showed up as your regular self. What to do about this? You can try to get them to take their power back. Gently deflect responsibility they try to bestow on you back onto them. Decline to offer your advice or opinion. Ask them what they think or what they would do instead. Point out to them the gifts that you see in them; do what you can to help them build up their own confidence. If none of these options work, you should try to stay as far away from them as you possibly can.

Early in her coaching career Madeleine worked with a number of law firms. She was hired to coach lawyers on developing their capacity to be rainmakers. In law firms *rainmaking* is the term used for building clientele and developing strong accounts. Many lawyers saw themselves as expert professionals and selling as beneath them. Yet some of the most talented lawyers in the firm were also great salespeople. The rainmakers were able to see the value that the law firm was creating and communicate that well to their clients, getting them to use legal services more extensively and strategically. In short, they were able to build trust and rapport with their clients and generate more billable hours.

Interestingly, Madeleine found that while the senior partners had a huge desire to grow rainmaking skills among their attorneys, an attorney who started to develop the ability to generate more business for the firm often experienced negative consequences. Her clients reported:

> "I finally brought in a new piece of business, and the partner yanks me off the account!"
> "Since I increased the monthly retainer, I've been branded as a troublemaker!"
> "You would have thought I lost the business rather than expanded it!"

Some were taken off key accounts by senior partners. Others received feedback from concerned coworkers that they were rocking the boat, and others heard that damaging things about their reputations were being whispered in hushed conversations. At first Madeleine was confused by this, until she realized that the negative consequences were reactions to the newfound successes. Some of the attorneys who found rainmaking to be difficult were threatened by the increasing success of others. Once it was figured out that the success was causing unintended consequences, the attorneys were able to develop strategies to manage the reactions of others.

When you learn to take responsibility for your gifts and abilities, you do not ratchet back your performance but rather figure out how to manage the impact of your gifts on others. In the case of the attorneys, they made sure that they kept the senior partners fully informed about all their activities and involved in any attempts to grow the business in the account. They focused on sharing the wealth with others and gave credit for anything anyone else did, no matter how small. By radically increasing communication and involvement they turned the fears of their colleagues and superiors into support.

It is of key importance that you take full responsibility for your gifts and stop waiting for the world to accept and praise you for them.

THE RULE OF CHOICE

The third rule of gifts is that just because you can do something well doesn't mean you should. One of the darkest aspects of gifts is the pressure they can exert. This became clear to Madeleine during a conversation with a friend many years ago. Liza, an extremely talented opera singer, was agonizing over her career. She had two small children and another on the way, and she had started a nanny service to generate much-needed income. She was upset because, as she put it, "God gave me this extraordinary voice, and I am not using it."

She deeply regretted not pursuing her singing career, and her nanny business didn't meet any of her current personal needs other than income. She was unable to assuage her guilt over not fulfilling what she had always thought was her destiny.

During the conversation Liza named the things that were truly important to her and examined her many other less dramatic but equally valuable gifts. She was able to put the gift of her voice in perspective; she would nurture it as much as she could, focusing on enjoying it rather than feeling obligated to *do* something with it.

Now Liza lives in Connecticut and runs a profitable nanny matching service while raising three beautiful children as a full-time mom. She sings for her church, a significant contribution that also offers her personal and public satisfaction. She no longer feels guilty about not being the opera superstar she once thought she should be.

Just because you can doesn't mean you should.

People think they are doing us a favor by telling us we are so good at something that we "should" be pursuing it as a career. But this is a mistake we see people make over and over again. In a groundbreaking book called *Do What You Love. The Money Will Follow,* Marsha Sinetar helps people work through the psychology of right livelihood, guiding them toward finding the work they are best suited for. The title of the book is incredibly powerful and has inspired people to make reckless decisions without reading the book! "Reckless" because the title is misleading in the case of entrepreneurs and artists. The book covers in detail what is involved in taking the risks necessary to build a life around work that does not automatically generate income and security. The book makes the important point that working as an entrepreneur or artist absolutely requires a head for business, some kind of financial backup system, and a decade's worth of patience and persistence. But the title is all some people hear, and this has led to some poor choices. All to point out that enjoying your gift does not necessarily imply that you should build a life or even a Prime Objective around it. In fact, that can be one sure way to kill the pleasure that some gifts provide.

Clarity regarding gifts is one of the greatest services that coaching can provide an individual. It helps you distinguish between the self-imposed standards of should/must and what you *choose* to focus on now. Clarity is what you will get from doing the exercise on page 98.

Choose one gift in particular from the list that you generated in the previous exercise. Best to choose one that causes some inner conflict. Do the same exercise for each of your gifts. Use the questions in the right-hand column below to guide you in answering the questions in the left-hand column. Write your answers in the left-hand column.

- Every gift is a double-edged sword. Be aware of the rewards and the dark side of each gift in order to fully leverage it.
- Even if you didn't ask for your gift, it is yours and therefore your responsibility to manage.
- Helping others to deal with and enjoy your gift doubles its value.

Leverage My Gifts Worksheet

My Gift: _____

Who else sees it?	Who has noticed this about me? Do they wish me well or not?
How does it affect others?	Do people encourage this gift of mine? Is it considered negative in some way in my environment? Do others consider it totally positive? Does it bother people? In what way? Does it inspire people? Does it cause jealousy in others? Does it make others uncomfortable?
How is it useful to me?	Has it gotten me things I am not sure I deserve? Will it help me achieve what I want? Does it bring me things others wish for but don't have?
How is it a burden?	Do I sometimes wish I didn't have this gift? Do I fantasize about being average? Am I jealous of people who do not have this gift?
In what ways do I deny or disown this gift?	Do I try to share it with others who don't want it? Do I try to teach others how to have the same gift because I don't want to be the only one around me with it because I feel guilty? Do I pretend that I do not have this gift when it is inconvenient? Do I sometimes wish I did not have it? Do I try to pretend it is not important that I have this gift? That it does not affect my life, or my success?
How do I leverage my gift to accomplish my primary objective?	Do I best leverage my gift in the achievement of my goals? Do I use my gift to get my needs met appropriately?
How do I nurture my gift?	Do I gently embrace and enjoy this gift without feeling guilty? Do I gracefully respond to others who admire my gift? Do I express gratitude for my gift regularly and with humility? Do I seek the company of others who understand the implications and full value of my gift? Do I seek to share my gift with others who have a great desire and willingness to appreciate and help me to leverage my gift without abusing it?
How will it get in my way?	Do I sometimes forget how my gift affects others? Do I take it for granted?
What will I do from now on to appreciate and leverage my gift to the best of my abilities?	Who will help me to be mindful of my gift? How will I remind myself to appreciate it?

CHAPTER SIX

Get Your Needs Met

How do you undermine yourself?

A personal need is that which you must have met to get to and maintain a peak state. Needs and your ability to get them met are a fundamental part of your coaching journey. We aren't talking about basic survival needs like food and shelter—we're referring to deeply personal, often emotional needs. Because needs *are* so personal, it can be hard to admit we have them. God forbid that we appear needy. Having needs can make us feel so terrifyingly vulnerable that we develop a habit of denying them even to ourselves, or if we are aware of them, of trying to hide them from others. But that we all have needs is a simple fact, an undeniable reality. It is also true that they cause much less trouble if they are identified and taken care of.

Trouble? How do needs cause trouble? By getting met, consciously or unconsciously—and productively or unproductively. Because needs simply *will* get met, you can make a choice to understand them well, or you can choose to let them rule your behavior in ways that take you (and others) by surprise. Let's be clear that the question is not "Do I get my needs met?" It is "*How* do I get my needs met?"

Ultimately your chance of achieving your Prime Objective only increases as you build your systems and community in such a way that your needs are well taken care of.

Snapshot:

Tim is the CEO of a small start-up company that has been in business for two years and is inching toward profitability. True to his temperament, Tim is getting bored with the small details involved in running the business, even though he is strongly committed to making the company successful. Next to Tim's many golf trophies and paintings of famous golf holes are framed Dilbert cartoon strips. He thinks Dilbert is hilarious because he has experienced being trapped in endless corporate politics, a hands-tied, nobody-make-a-decision-so-we-can-all-just-fly-under-the-radar world. He escaped that nightmare just in time.

Tim recognizes that he has a need for expediency and forthrightness, but sometimes he forgets. He has just finished a conversation with his VP of sales who is angry again that Tim just cut a really creative deal with a client, rolling over and barreling through all the protocols the entire leadership team has agreed to. Their communication has gone from bad to terrible; Tim practically hung up on her. He had expected at least some positive response; after all he did make an excellent, sorely needed sale. Tim is annoyed with his VP, but worse, he feels lousy about himself because he knows he is shooting himself by once again angering a valuable team member.

Tim, though, has had the experience of working with a coach and knows about needs. He asks himself the dead-giveaway needs question: "When I behave in a way that I don't respect or that does not serve me, what need am I getting met?"

Ah! Of course! His need for expediency will get him every time. He realizes that this need, compounded by his recent boredom, is indicative of a need to shift his role in the company, directing his attention more squarely on rainmaking than on day-to-day management. He begins to *plan for significant changes in how he will function within his company; he has no idea how relieved his senior team will be.*

Let's face it. Most of us didn't have a lot of great role models of people who persistently and graciously got their personal needs met. What we did have were models of people who got their needs met in ways that were perceived as pushy, whiny, or shrill. *Selfish.* We hear others talking about these people, and we think, *Oh, well, no one is going to be saying that about me.*

From an early age many of us learn to dismiss our needs, afraid we will appear selfish or rude, uncooperative, lacking in team spirit. We often view our habit of dismissing needs as a useful or even healthy one; we've gotten this far after all. However, dismissing needs gets you only so far and no farther.

In order to function at the kind of level you demand of yourself without burning out, you will simply have to give yourself permission to get your needs met—to be *selfish*—but in a way that won't alienate your friends or diminish your influence. The paradox you will discover is that as you understand yourself, others will find it easier to understand you. They will help you more often than not. Linda Berens, an expert on psychological types and the way personality differences affect relationships, has this to say about needs: "The Needs represent . . . the driving force. Individuals unconsciously and consciously seek every avenue to get the Needs met. When these Needs are met the individual is energized and light of spirit. When these Needs are not met, the individual is drained of energy and suffers dissatisfaction or stress."

Drained of energy? Dissatisfied in some unidentifiable way? Sound familiar? Let's examine what you can do about it.

The first step is to identify your needs. Identifying needs requires some sleuthing and is more straightforward for some than for others. Some people have maintained their commitment to appearing "needless" for so long that they have convinced themselves that they have no needs. If this sounds like you, you may be wanting to skip this chapter altogether. Resist that impulse, because your denial will eventually catch up to you. This is your chance to nip it in the bud. If you have some idea of what your needs are but have developed the very common habit of ignoring them or covering them up, you have some work to do.

Once you have identified what your needs are, the next step is to give yourself permission to have them. They are yours. Whether you came hardwired with them or developed them over time is not up for debate here. They are yours and there is no getting around it. Giving yourself permission to own your needs is crucial. For many, their coach is the first person in their life who gives them this permission. So we, as your coaches right now, give you that permission. If that doesn't work for you, answer this: just who do you need permission from? If you are old enough to be reading this book, the only person you need permission from is staring back at you when you look in the mirror. Think about it. And remember this: you can do it now or later, but you'll eventually want to do it.

Once permission is granted, you will develop a plan to get your needs met. You can handle them one at a time if you need to take it slow or a couple at a time. Your plan will require practice. Learning how to get needs met takes practice and a fair amount of dedication and persistence. The first couple of attempts you make may not work as you had planned. You can't quit at the first sign of resistance. You'll need the support of people you trust.

If the prospect of enlisting help makes you crazy, go back to Chapter Four and read the section "Identify the Players." Getting where you are going on your own won't happen, can't happen, so give it up right now. Or you might be thinking that you've disguised your needs effectively, and you are not about to reveal them to anyone. Forget it. Everybody sees them anyway. They are either politely looking away or teasing you behind your back, so you might just as well get it all out in the open.

Whether you are in deep denial or simply covering up, *"What are you trying to hide?"* is the question to ask yourself. This question is directly connected to the Third Perspective: How do you want to be seen? *We cannot hide our needs.* In fact, the harder we try, the more obvious they become and the more vulnerable we are.

When someone with a need to have their hard work noticed goes sniffing around for acknowledgment, they might be getting a need met, but it would be much easier for everyone around them if they would just ask for it directly. You might have a need for admiration that expresses itself as conflict avoidance—in your need to be admired as a nice person, you may simply forego arguing about anything. Or perhaps you are reluctant to make decisions that may disappoint someone else and so make no decisions. In the end, nobody wins. In the end, things just get boring or frustrating for all concerned.

We have seen the need for predictability and preparation cause people to hound colleagues and cause annoying clashes. We've watched people who have the need for individual accomplishment struggle in situations where group success is paramount; those needs can lead to frustration. The list is endless, but fortunately only a few are particular to you. Each of your needs influences your behavior and attitudes and can cause no end of frustration when it remains unacknowledged. Recognize your needs, and figure out how to treat them in ways that contribute to your strength, well-being, and greater success in your environment.

▓ A BRIEF HISTORY OF NEEDS ▓

Abraham Maslow established a now widely accepted theory that all human beings have a hierarchy of needs, which must be met in a specific order. His work has flowed into the zeitgeist the way Freud's notion of the unconscious has. His view of humans is more optimistic than Freud's. According to Maslow humans are hardwired to satisfy basic needs for shelter, air, food, and water. Once those have been satisfied, people are free to then seek stability and safety in their lives; this is generally represented by a strong and safe family unit. Then, when people feel safe and stable, the next natural impulse is to seek groups in which to feel accepted and build camaraderie. This is the need for belonging. Then and only then are people free to meet their esteem needs, which usually take the form of competence or mastery. There is overlap between the need to belong and the esteem needs. Humans naturally seek to belong to groups that recognize their accomplishments. The last need in Maslow's hierarchy is self-actualization, or the deep desire to maximize one's potential. Self-actualization often takes the form of a search for knowledge, a life devoted to God, and what we generally think of as self-fulfillment. The hierarchy looks like this:

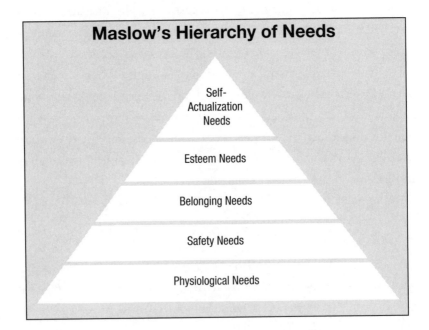

Maslow's Hierarchy of Needs

Self-Actualization Needs

Esteem Needs

Belonging Needs

Safety Needs

Physiological Needs

There is a good chance that you have the first two or even three, moving from the bottom of the pyramid up, pretty much covered. There are myriad social programs to assist people in their quest to meet the needs in the bottom tier. The creation of coaching as a profession was essentially a response to the number of people who are actively seeking to meet their esteem and self-actualization needs. The percentage of people free to address these needs is higher now than at any time in modern history, and we are just beginning as a culture to understand these needs and provide multiple avenues for people to get them met. Coaching appeared in response to the deep desire by many to think more deeply about relationships and make finer distinctions to better express ourselves.

▪ GETTING PAST THE OBSTACLES ▪

Once people have identified their needs, there are often self-imposed obstacles to getting them met. Why self-imposed? Because they are the direct result of how people see themselves, how they believe others see them, how they want to be seen, and their own diehard beliefs about what constitutes effective behavior. We've heard just about every reason there is. What are yours?

Taking the Needs Mini-Scrubdown can shed some light on your beliefs and thought patterns. In the section beyond, you will find a brief discussion that will help you to shift your perspective a bit. As with the other Scrubdowns, simply circle the letters T or F to mark each statement *true* or *false*.

The Needs Mini-Scrubdown

1. I was raised not to ask for help.   T   F
2. I don't deserve to get my need met.   T   F
3. My need is too expensive.   T   F
4. I want to believe that I am "cool."   T   F
5. I wouldn't want to spoil myself—I might get too soft.   T   F
6. I don't want to be like _____.   T   F
7. My need is inconvenient.   T   F
8. My need does not fit with how I want others to see me.   T   F
9. I am terrified that _____ will judge me selfish.   T   F
10. I have no idea how to get my need met without attracting
    negative attention to myself.   T   F

We all have our reasons for ignoring our needs—solid, valid reasons that have served us well. And we all know that human beings can put up with enormous amounts of pain and deprivation. In the case of the pain caused by not getting your needs met, the key question would be *Why?* Why do you deprive yourself when the cost is so enormous? Let's take a look at which items you marked as *true.* If your answers are concentrated in a specific area, please feel free to skip ahead to the area that addresses you.

Statements 1–3: **How you see yourself**
If you answered *true* mainly to the first three questions, your resistance to getting your needs met is coming from the environment in which you were raised. If you see yourself as strictly a self-sufficient person, it is time to reconsider just what you are going to accomplish by yourself. Or perhaps you don't think you matter that much.

If that is the case, we would ask you to consider: who matters more than you? Even if you have many people who matter more to you than yourself, chances are those people depend on you—they'll want and need you to be at your best.

Has someone who had to remain extremely stoic in the face of adversity heavily influenced you? Many cultures are steeped in the pride of self-sufficiency. Those of us who come from a people who struggled furiously to get the first three levels in Maslow's hierarchy of needs met (physiological, safety, and belonging) often build environments in which the top two tiers (esteem and self-actualization) are considered to be inconsequential or even self-indulgent. If this is true for you, it is time to contrast your life and circumstances with theirs and adjust accordingly. Remember that every generation has an entirely new set of challenges.

Statements 4–6: **How others see you**

If you have a reputation for being a tower of strength, there is a good chance you are now deeply invested in the image. Keeping up with your own reputation is not always a worthy pursuit. Ask yourself how maintaining a particular image might be costing you in ways you can't afford. If image maintenance isn't an issue for you, you may have fallen into the habit of being strong merely because you have a high threshold for stress. In Chapter Five, Manage Your Gifts, we discussed the principle *Just because you can do something doesn't mean you should.* One of the biggest impediments to getting needs met is the ability to bear stress. Although handy in a crisis, this is not necessarily a good thing in long-term day-to-day living, because it keeps you from knowing that a need is not being met until you have reached a breaking point. If you are very strong and resilient and can tolerate immense amounts of stress, check in with yourself early and often. Tell yourself the truth about what you are experiencing. *The back of even the strongest camel will break if the load becomes too heavy.*

Statements 7–9: **How you want to be seen**

How we want to be seen can keep us from ever getting our needs met. This brings to mind the old line "Don't mind me, I'll just sit here in the dark," the plaintive cry of the elderly mother who is simply dying for attention, the one who makes everyone roll their eyes because she is so transparent. The more we get our needs met, the less needy we are. By denying our needs and thus making ourselves feel "strong," we make our needs transparently obvious to others.

We've all heard about people who exhibit all the symptoms of cardiac failure but deny the obvious because they don't want to "be a bother." This is an extreme example, yet it points out to what extremes some will go to avoid appearing selfish. We are horrified by examples in our own families or characters from literature who were so selfish that they sucked the life from everyone around them. We would rather die of a heart attack than be like them.

Statement 10: **You don't know how**

Welcome to the club. If we all knew how to get our needs met effectively, we'd be doing it, wouldn't we? Asking for help seems to be one of the hardest things for most of us to do. There are specific reasons why we hate to ask for help. How many of us grew up hearing variations on the adage "If you want something done right, do it yourself"?

On the other hand, Madeleine's mentor Thomas Leonard used to say, "Anything worth doing is worth getting help with." Think about how different your approach might be with this helpful shift in your point of view. For starters, it affords you a world of permission and possibility. The world of "do it yourself" is small and narrow—by its very nature limited.

"But people might say no," you say.

"But they might judge me. . . ."

"But that person might fail me. . . ."

All true. You have experienced all of the above. But that can't stop you. Meet Julie, and see how she does it.

Snapshot:

Julie is flying down the hallway with her equipment bag slamming on her hip. She is at least twenty minutes late for a meeting with a client—she has relied on an outdated train schedule. As she pushes through the door she sees her partner, Jack, talking animatedly on the phone, oblivious to the other three lines blinking madly.

"Where the hell is the new assistant?" Julie's voice sounds shrill to her own ears.

She needs to call her client, and she won't even get a line out at this rate. She drops her bag and rips open her current work drawer where the client's proofs are supposed to be. The file called Red Hook is missing. Julie feels her jaw tighten a fraction more as her shoulders creep dangerously close to her ears.

Her calendar for the day, which has the phone number of her client, should be on her desk but isn't. And where is the new assistant? Julie has the involuntary image of herself as a cartoon cat with its eyes bugging out of its head.

Jack hangs up the phone and walks into Julie's office, smiling and saying "Good news—" but he is cut off by a sound as loud as an air horn blast: "Well, I don't think—what's her name—Cami, Candi, whatever—not being here is good news. This place is a disaster; my conference call is not set up. Why do we pay her? And the bloody file is gone. My calendar with clients' numbers on it is missing. This place is a hellhole. I cannot go on working this way."

During Julie's tirade Jack steps back and says, "Whoa, I guess you got out of bed on the wrong side. I was about to tell you that I sent Cindy down to the Film Center because they finally got the tape we need for the Kruger job. That was her"—he points to the phone—*"telling me that she's got it and is on her way back." He stops and looks at Julie. "I think she's working out fine. When you come down from your diva fit, you can apologize to me. That is if I still feel like talking to you."*

Jack walks out shaking his head.

Julie sits at her desk wondering what happened. She knows she used to be fun and easy to work with. She can't figure out when she turned into a complete bitch.

Julie is clearly not herself. Later that day, she confides to her friend Jon. "I just hate who I am becoming," she moans. Her friend, who usually tries not to butt in, asks, "Why don't we talk about this some more?"

"You don't mind?" she asks softly.

"Not at all."

"We worked so hard to get the business off the ground, you know, and now everyone thinks we're great, but there is way too much going on, and I am completely overwhelmed." Julie just lets it all out in one long breath.

"Uh-huh," says her friend.

"All I ever wanted was to be a photographer, to take incredibly cool pictures of unusual structures and work with Jack, who is a genius. Lo and behold, people love our work, and not only that, who knew that I'd have such a fantastic head for marketing? I have everything I ever wanted, except now Jack thinks I am Dragon Lady and avoids me, I can't keep up with the schedule, and it's all going to hell in a fast car," Julie says, feeling embarrassingly close to tears.

"Uh-huh," says her friend.

"I can't do it, Jon, I can't keep up. I'm going to wreck everything because I can't handle the stress."

"That's crap," says Jon. "I've known you for twenty years, and if anybody can handle stress it's you. We both know you can handle stress. So what is it exactly that you really can't handle?"

His question is met with silence and then still more silence.

"Julie, what makes you go berserk?"

Silence again.

"The mess and the chaos," breathes Julie.

"Right. What have you done in the past when things feel out of control and too messy to manage? I've seen you do it. Think."

"I get my ducks in a row, and I knock 'em down one at a time," says Julie in a reflective voice; clearly she is thinking back. "I swing into action and put things in order and boss people around until they help me."

Jon laughs; he's seen it. "Yes, and everyone is happier because when you decide to clean things up, every dust bunny in town runs for its life. And come on, I'm sure Jack would love to have you happy and productive again."

"But I'm such a slave driver when I get that way."

"Effective slave driver or scatterbrained diva from hell, which would you pick? And by the way, successful businesspeople have to maintain high standards."

"So should I get another assistant, someone who can work just for me?"

"That's an idea. It sounds like there might be too much work for one. So what are you going to do?"

"Hold on, I'm hatching a plot. . . ." Julie is so excited she can't wait to get off the phone and work on her plan.

Julie needs order. She has always been extremely precise and organized in her affairs, but her business is growing so fast that things have spun out of control. Like most things in life, it happened incrementally, and she didn't even see it. At first, Julie blames herself instead of examining the circumstances that provoked the situation. She needs a step-by-step process or conversation to help her identify her deeply personal need. Next, Julie has to understand that having a need does not make her weak or high maintenance; her fear is of being a burden. What she now realizes is that without the order she needs, she is far more of a burden. Getting her need for order met helps everyone lighten up.

Julie is then inspired to design a plan to get her needs met in a way that doesn't make her look bad or needy. Her next step is to communicate her discoveries to the important people in her life and enlist their help. Finally, Julie will vigilantly watch for any other unmet needs that may arise as she forges ahead.

Back to Julie:

Julie walks into the office a few days after the blowup. Jack is sitting at his desk reviewing a proposal. He looks up at her over his glasses with one eyebrow cocked. It's clear he doesn't know what to expect.

"I owe you an apology," says Julie. "I was a diva, and I lost my cool. I'm really sorry, and I promise never to do it again."

Jack is pleasantly surprised. "Thanks," he says. "What's going on with you, anyway?"

"After a lot of thought, I realized that as we've become more successful, the basics here in the office have become more chaotic. I don't have the time to put things in order, to have this place precisely organized in the way I need it to be to function well."

Jack laughs. "Yes, we all know you're a card-carrying member of control freaks anonymous. Can't you get over that?" Julie suppresses her annoyance at his cavalier attitude.

"Listen, I really want things to go smoothly and for us to do great work together. I was trying to get over it. You saw what happened. Hear me out on my proposal."

Julie lays out a plan to hire another assistant just to take care of her schedule and keep her organized. Jack agrees that with her workload it makes sense. They talk about Julie's days in the office, not on location, and the importance of her setting aside the last half hour of the day to clear her desk, plan for the next morning, and assemble the materials she'd be using throughout the following day. That means Julie won't be available for any of the conference calls Jack prefers scheduling late in the day.

"This seems so stupid, to have to spend time hashing this stuff out," says Julie. "It seems so picky."

"Yeah, it does," says Jack, "but if it'll make you happy, it'll be worth it."

"Thanks." Julie smiles. "Let's give this plan a shot and see how things go. We'll check in in a couple of weeks."

Julie found that it was far easier to accept her need for order than to deny it. Julie was not defective. She was simply not recognizing and acknowledging a fundamental aspect of herself. She is now able to show up in the world exactly as she sees herself: organized, respectful of others, on time, able to keep her word, and productive. By denying her need for order, she appeared exactly the opposite of how she saw herself.

How can you do the same? By following the same process that Julie did.

1. **Identify and articulate specific highly personal needs**. We will help you by providing a list of potential needs for you to consider. Some may have already occurred to you. One of the best ways is to think back to a recent time when you felt you were simply not yourself. This would be a moment in which you behaved in a way that you don't condone or are ashamed of because you know it didn't represent the real you. Ask yourself: what need was not getting met?

2. **Give yourself permission**. We talked earlier about giving yourself permission. One of the prime motivators for doing so comes from recognizing that not giving in and admitting to a need will end up hurting you more in the long term. Julie could see the

cost of her denial because it caused a crisis. You may want to give yourself permission before a crisis occurs.

3. **Identify the people in your life who can help.** Julie was either smart or lucky; she talked it over with someone she trusted, who knew her well and was a good listener. He helped her to think through her situation and asked good questions. It is a really good idea to cultivate relationships with people who can do this for you, and you can return the favor. It was clear to Julie that she really disturbed her partner—the very person she needed help from. To get help, she needed to apologize and admit what was bothering her.

4. **Set a goal and choose activities to move you toward it.** It is much easier to come up with solutions once the problem is clear. Often a plan will come as a blinding flash of the obvious because, as we noted earlier, the obstacles to getting needs met are usually self-imposed. We offer a template for building your plan in The Needs Exercise on page 115.

5. **Anticipate what could go wrong**. Although needs stay the same, circumstances change—often rapidly. Even the most competent people can get caught up in the whirlwind of events. It is easy to miss changes that can cause a need to become unmet. Consider major events in light of your needs—anticipate what could go wrong and make arrangements before a crisis occurs.

Here is a question many people ask: what if I pick the wrong need to work on? A valid concern. The answer is you really can't go wrong. Learning how to get your needs met is like learning any new habit—it takes some trial and error. Anything you learn as you get one need met will help you with others. Resist the impulse to pick one that feels impossible—don't sabotage yourself that way. If you have been working with a therapist for ten years to get your need for love met by your mother and have not yet succeeded, this is not the magic bullet. Choose to work on a need that you suspect will make an impact on your quality of life and start with that. For example, you may be struggling with a frustrating mismatch with a colleague at work, like the VP of sales in our opening snapshot who had a need for precision and sequential order that was at odds with her boss's need to get to the point. Often what we interpret as "severe personality differences" is the aggravation of two conflicting unmet needs.

▦ THE NEEDS EXERCISE ▦

Step One. Consider

What specifically was driving you the last time you behaved in a way that was contrary to the way you see yourself or in a way that made you feel embarrassed and ashamed?

⮞ What was happening?

_____

⮞ How did you feel afterward?

_____

⮞ What need was not getting met?

_____

⮞ What might you have done differently to get your need met?

_____

⮞ Whom might you discuss this with who might offer or lead you to some insight?

_____

Step Two. Identify

Circle the words that strike you as a need. Think about what you must have to be at your best.

To have clarity	To accomplish	To be respected	To make sure rules are
To be recognized	To build a legacy	To be adored	followed
To be a master	To get things done	To have variety	To have freedom to
To be competent	To have influence	To have control over	do what you
To make an impact	To create	others	please
To fulfill duty	To express feelings	To have control over	To have freedom from
To be responsible	To interpret the work of	events	restrictions imposed
To have harmony	others	To have self-control	by others
To have peace	To be ethical	To have discipline	To label
To have justice	To be moral	To have data	To categorize
To have fairness	To be honest	To have information	To catalog
To be able to trust	To be truthful	To have knowledge	To serve society
To be trustworthy	To see the silver	To be accurate	To help people
To have fun	lining	To have power over	To help animals
To have physical	To see the dark side	oneself	To be right
pleasure	To belong to a group	To have power over	To be an expert
To have joy	To be certain	others	To have a unique identity
To have humor	To be in action	To be accepted	To have meaning
To be spiritual	To reflect	To be included	To have significance
To have entitlement	To have adventure	To innovate	To feel connected to
To have permission	To court danger	To buck the system	people
To have solitude	To be a player	To be a rebel	To feel connected to
To have quiet	To be a part of things	To be an iconoclast	issues
To have balance	To perform well	To challenge authority	To have intimacy
To have order	To be cared for	To break rules	To have safety
To have opportunity	To be well regarded	To make rules	To feel secure

Step Three. Compile

Make a list of what you circled:

1. _____

2. _____

3. _____

4. _____

5. _____

6. _____

7. _____

8. _____

Step Four. Whittle Down

Choose *three* words from the above list that feel/sound/look like the most pressing needs *right now.*

1. _____

What happens to you when this need is not met?

What behaviors do you exhibit when this need is not met?

What does it cost you (in terms of the respect of others) when this
    need is not met?

How would your life be different if this need were permanently
    met?

2. _____

What happens to you when this need is not met?

What behaviors do you exhibit when this need is not met?

What does it cost you (in terms of the respect of others) when this
    need is not met?

How would your life be different if this need were permanently
met?

3. _____

What happens to you when this need is not met?

What behaviors do you exhibit when this need is not met?

What does it cost you (in terms of the respect of others) when this
need is not met?

How would your life be different if this need were permanently
met?

Step Five. Be Brutal

Choose the one need that seems most compelling to you right
now—that most intrigues you and the one you need the most
help with. You really can't go wrong. The only error you can
make is not to choose and quit here. You are better than that—
you know at least one need that you could work on.

4. _____

Are you willing to set a goal and commit to getting this need
met within a certain time frame?

If *yes* move ahead; if *no* go to Step Nine.

Step Six. Set a Goal

What goal can you set that will get this need met, once and for
all? Or at least get the need met for a long period of time, until
things change?

You will want this goal to be *specific* and *measurable*. This
sounds easy but may require a few tries. All research about
goals shows that specificity is powerful. Ask yourself: how will
know if I've reached it? What will be the measure of my success? Assign a date to your goal—it will keep you from being

vague and allowing yourself to procrastinate. It will also force you to put your activities into a time line. You can use the same backward planning technique that was covered in Chapter Two.

Write the goal: _____

By when? _____

Step Seven. Brainstorm

Answer the following questions to help you determine what actions you can take to achieve your goal:

➤ Do you already know exactly what would meet your need? (If *yes* skip to Step Eight. If *no* continue.)

➤ Who in your life knows, loves, or cares about you in a nonjudgmental way with whom you might brainstorm ideas of how you can get this need met?

➤ Imagine what your life would look like if your need were met. If you could wave a magic wand to get your need met *right now*, how would things be? What would the picture look like? What clues are there in your picture?

➤ Consider others who might have a similar need. What do they do to get it met?

Step Eight. Get Help

Who in your life might be able to help you with this?

1. _____

2. _____

How might you ask (person 1) _____ to (specific action) _____ ?

I will ask (person 1) _____ by
(date) _____ .

How might you ask (person 2) _____ to
(specific action) _____ ?
I will ask (person 2) _____ by
(date) _____ .

What other actions will you take? By when?
_____ by _____
_____ by _____
_____ by _____
_____ by _____

Step Nine. Inspiration

If you are feeling that this is more difficult than you expected, consider the following:

- What gets in the way of your asking for what you need?
- What are you missing by not sharing crucial information with this person?
- Has it occurred to you that it might hurt or annoy them that you never share this kind of information with them?
- Who are you *really* taking care of by *not* asking for what you need?
- How does this serve them or you?
- What behavior traits or characteristics of yours create problems for you? What are you willing to do to address those aspects of yourself?
- What problems really belong to someone else that you are trying to solve by denying your own need?

➠ Does it help you to hope that someone will figure it out? Are you secretly hoping that people around you will become mind readers?

➠ What is the cost to you of continually putting on a fixed expression every time you relinquish an opportunity to ask for what you need?

➠ How is it helping you to not express specifically what you need?

➠ What behaviors do you engage in that you do not approve of that you could eliminate by getting your need met?

➠ What does it cost you when you behave in way that you do not understand or cannot control?

➠ What will it eventually cost you to not get this need met?

Congratulations. You have begun the process of understanding what your personal needs are and how you might get them met. Start with one or two. Once a few start getting taken care of, it gets easier and easier. Getting your needs met is an ongoing, cyclical process. The key is aquiring the *habit* of getting your needs met.

- Having needs isn't a problem; not taking care of them is.
- Needs will get themselves met regardless of how much you ignore them. It is much better to get your needs met appropriately than run the risk of having them surface unexpectedly in situations you can't control.
- You can't hide your needs; everyone sees them anyway.
- Identify your needs and plan when and how to get them met.
- Ask for guidance from others in getting your needs met. You might be surprised at how willing they are to help!

CHAPTER SEVEN

Cherish and Protect
Your Valuables

■ ▼ ■

What really matters to you?

Once you know what your needs are and how to get them met, getting a handle on your valuables will add a turbo boost. We define a valuable as something that is precious to you. You can live without what is precious, but it sure isn't fun. Valuables are the cream in your coffee, the champagne of life—the more you can design your life to enjoy as many of them as possible, the more energy you will have. Do you know what matters most to you? Are you really sure? You may assume you know, but what if you are wrong? You may define what's important based on what your parents, grandparents, or teachers believe. It is crucial to know because the decisions you make on a moment-to-moment basis depend largely on what matters most to you. What is valuable to you will color every choice you make whether you are aware of it or not.

Snapshot:

Ravi loves his job. When he moved to the United States, he applied for and won a dream position in information technology. He gets to spend all day writing code and solving technical problems for people who need his help. Troubleshooting is his passion. When his clients see him charging down their hallways, they breathe a sigh of relief. Ravi is too young to remember the early TV westerns. If he did, he would know to sound the cavalry bugle each time he arrives on the scene.

Until a year ago, the company he worked for was committed to Ravi's continued learning and development. However, after the company underwent severe cuts, all training was suspended.

Yesterday Ravi ran into a client problem he didn't know how to solve because he had not yet been trained in that area. He tried a few work-arounds and quickly realized he was wasting his and his client's time. He apologized and said he would be back in the afternoon with more information. Ravi left feeling frustrated and disappointed. He remembered reading something about the nature of the problem in a trade magazine. With his current workload he didn't have the time to find it. He called his new manager and left a voice mail message about a need for further training. He didn't hear back.

Ravi went to his office where he found a slew of e-mails and voice mails. There was not enough time or staff to deal with all the emergencies coming in, some of which were caused by new software installations. The afternoon came and went, and he was never able get back to his morning client. Finally at 9:00 P.M. he left for home, feeling out of sorts and unusually pensive.

Ravi got calls from headhunters at least once a week, and for the first time, he considered listening to what they had to say. He didn't mind the hours or the hard work in his current job, but he didn't feel that he was being equipped to solve the latest glitches and problems. He missed seeing the relieved smiles on his clients' faces.

Being equipped with the solutions and answers that let him stay ahead of his customers' needs is *valuable* to Ravi. When his company stopped his training he was no longer able to prepare himself and so he is losing something that is *valuable* to him. Ravi is just beginning to pay for this loss. Fortunately, once we understand that a valuable is not being honored, the action required to fix the situation is often easy to see. Ravi must find a way to be prepared to solve his customers' problems or reconcile himself to constant frustration. No wonder he is considering leaving his job!

Valuables are what we cherish and hold dear. As we see with Ravi, the things we find valuable are unique and critically important to us. The things we value shape and guide the way we act, the decisions we make, and how we feel about our quality of life. We shape statements or rules surrounding those things that we find valuable. In Ravi's case, he values being able to solve his clients' problems efficiently. Ravi's valuables are preparation, expertise, but above all, customer satisfaction.

■ WHAT'S IN A NAME? ■

So why do we use the term *valuables,* instead of values? What is the point? We went out of our way to change the word for a couple of reasons. First, the word *values* is loaded with a lot of weighty definitions. Values are statements or codes of conduct that come from religions, societies, institutions, ethnicities, cultures, families, companies, Boy Scout troops, you name it. Everywhere you turn there are groups of people telling us how we should conduct ourselves. In contrast, valuables are those things that *you* find valuable. Valuables are all about you and your life.

The second reason we use the term *valuables* is that values provoke strong emotions, feelings, reactions, and judgments toward others and ourselves. Since every social institution we encounter espouses values, they often invoke strong feelings that can confuse us or color what we truly hold as valuable. Values tell us what we should or should not do. Some people don't mind being told what to do; others rebel. In either case values are imposed by something external.

With *valuables,* we attempt to strip away the moral or ethical context of values and whatever feelings we have about them. We believe that when you look closely at your personal valuables, as you will in this chapter, it is useful to ditch as much emotional baggage as possible. If you are going to learn how to cherish and protect your valuables, you'll want to be sure they are yours. To do this you'll need to get as objective a view of yourself as you can, so you can decide what stays, what goes, and what gets added to your new and improved list of valuables.

There are a few useful distinctions and definitions to clarify the concept of valuables. The leader in the field of values is Milton Rokeach, who began his work on the subject over thirty years ago. It still impresses us with its simplicity, elegance, and usefulness. In Rokeach's own words:

> to say that a person "has a value" is to say that he/she has an enduring belief that a specific mode of conduct or end-state of existence is personally or socially preferable to alternate codes of conduct or end-states of existence. Once a value is internalized it becomes, consciously or unconsciously, a standard or criterion for guiding action, for developing and maintaining attitudes toward relevant objects or situations, for justifying one's own and others' actions and attitudes, for morally judging self and others, and for comparing self to others. Finally, a value is a standard employed to influence the values and attitudes and actions of at least some others—our children's, for example.

Rokeach's statement on values provides a great opportunity for in-depth exploration and thought. Essentially, he said that our values:

⟹ Are enduring. Though they may shift over a lifetime, they do not change as easily as do attitudes and beliefs.

⟹ Come in two categories: *means values and ends values*. We have changed Rokeach's words to make the idea easier to use: *daily living* valuables define how things should be done on a daily basis, and *destination* valuables define the way we want things to become in the end.

⟹ Become set or internalized. Once that happens, they become the basic criteria we use to judge, evaluate, behave, justify, and compare ourselves and others.

⟹ Influence others, at work and at home, especially our children.

Valuables can be diamonds as big as the Ritz with real importance, or they can be tiny cut-glass baubles that give us small but meaningful pleasure. Valuables are the things you care about and pay attention to when it doesn't matter what anyone else thinks. There are actually people in the world, and you might be one of them, who keep their homes spotless even when they are not expecting guests. Neatness and cleanliness are valuables to them.

Ask yourself: if I were down to my last five dollars until payday, what would I spend it on? Would it be flowers for myself or bleach for the linens or ice cream for my sweetie? Does the milk money get blown on cigars or ballet slippers?

There's no right answer; they are all right. Each person accumulates a treasure trove of valuables, whether they are objects, sensory perceptions, emotional states, or experiences with an elemental importance that may (or may not) outweigh their intrinsic worth. Elegance, accuracy, fun, creativity, luxury, simplicity—these are a few of the more abstract valuables.

While valuables differ greatly from person to person, each human being generally has a long list of valuables, and they fall into two distinct categories: *daily living* and *destination valuables*. Every moment of every day we use our valuables to decide what we should and should not do and what others should and should not do.

Daily living valuables serve as a compass. Why does John yield and let another driver easily enter his lane while his wife, Megan, just looks ahead and hits the accelerator? A difference in the importance of the valuable of courtesy is likely the reason. Why does Megan stay in touch with friends from college and John let himself fall out of touch with his college buddies? Megan has a strong valuable of maintaining connections and John doesn't. Our daily living valuables inform and direct the actions we take in every circumstance whether we are aware of it or not.

Why does Marshal plan to end his career at sixty and move down south for a life of golf and leisure while Richard plans to keep his nose to the grindstone well into his seventies with no intention of retiring even though he has the financial resources to retire anytime? A difference in the destination valuable of work. One person has a clear destination valuable of golf, fishing, and leisure in his golden years while the other has achieved his destination valuable already. Richard has a destination valuable of hard work and contribution, and therefore the idea of retiring doesn't even enter his thinking.

We all have a unique collection of both daily living and destination valuables. Many of the people we have worked with over the years have never acknowledged or celebrated their valuables, let alone brought them out and used them in ways that give them pleasure and nourish them. Once we know our valuables and take ownership of them every day, we are more likely to feel as if our lives are under control and headed in the right direction. Our choices and actions begin to feel more right to us. When we lack clarity about what our valuables are, or neglect to take them into account, we slowly and surely lose our enjoyment and energy.

Focus on Jack:

Remember Jack, Julie's partner from the previous chapter? As Jack watched Julie work hard to get her needs met, he realized that all was not right with him either. He really wanted to change something about their office environment. He thought about it a little and saw that their dingy entryway really brought down his mood. He and Julie had agreed that someday they would fix it up. Jack went to talk to Julie about this forgotten agreement.

"Jules, I need to talk to you about something that's important to me."

"What's up?" asked Julie. She was reviewing her calendar for the day while gathering her equipment.

"I've been watching you get it together to destress your work life, and it occurs to me that a little part of me dreads coming here every day."

Julie's eyes widened. She stopped working and sat down. "No kidding, I had no idea. It's not because I'm such a whack job, is it?"

Jack laughed, waving away that suggestion. "No, no. I knew that going in, hon. Do you remember how we agreed that we would fix up the entryway? We didn't actually say when we would do it, and I'm not even sure what we can afford, but I think the time has come. It's beginning to bug me, a lot. It's dingy and pathetic, and I don't think it represents us well to our clients."

"Wow, Jack, I don't even notice it. I'm not sure we can afford the extra expense right now."

"Right, I know, but we are doing well. I'd be willing to risk a small investment. I know exactly how it should look, and my friend Richard can help us do it inexpensively. I'd like to get your input on the ideas and your approval to go ahead and spend some money on it."

Julie remembered Jack's support for her rearrangement of office procedures and his approval of another assistant. She could tell how important this was to Jack; it was rare that they sat down long enough to go over schedules, let alone discuss something as mundane as the decor of the entryway. It made sense; Jack's apartment was a jewel of perfection, photographs of it were continually appearing in magazines, and her friends always went to him for decorating advice. "Jack," she said, "that's cool. Just let me know what you want to do, what you think it will cost, and what you need me to do to help. I've never noticed the entryway, but this is clearly important to you, and if it makes you feel better, it'll pay off in the long run."

Jack walked away from the conversation glowing with the excitement of how fantastic it was going to be to rip down the ugly brown paneling that had bothered him from day one.

What are your valuables? Is it essential to you to be sincere or is reason paramount? What destinations do you desire? Do you seek freedom or do you seek security? Is it both? Sometimes valuables can seem to conflict with one another. In those cases, you have confused daily living valuables with destination valuables. For example, some people find security to be valuable as a destination (retire to someplace warm and sunny), whereas others think of security, specifically financial security, as a route to the destination of having the freedom to travel as they please.

Many of our valuables are evident but not well articulated. When we can describe our valuables clearly and succinctly, it makes it much easier to act on them and communicate them to others. As Milton Rokeach said, "an adult has tens of thousands of beliefs, thousands of attitudes, but only dozens of values. A value system is a hierarchical organization—a rank ordering—of ideals or values in terms of importance. To one person truth, beauty and freedom may be at the top of the list, and thrift, order and cleanliness at the bottom; to another person, the order may be reversed."

The Valuables activity below will help you understand and name the valuables that most influence your behavior. We are going to ask you to go through the list and determine the five most critical valuables from each category: the daily living valuables of conduct or behavior that form the basis for your standards and the destination valuables of the end state that probably influence your Prime Objective.

Before we go to the list, we must return to the Three Perspectives from Chapter Three for just a minute. While our valuables are connected to the Three Perspectives—How do I see myself? How do others see me? and How do I want to be seen?—valuables are especially important in considering the Third Perspective. Our valuables, to a large extent, take shape in our early childhood under the influence of our parents and the people who raised us. We are governed by the valuables formed during these early life relationships until our early adulthood, when there is a shift. Around age thirty-five or so, many adults break away from their parents' valuables hierarchy and begin to sense their own emerging, unique set of valuables. As you sort through these, pay attention to how yours differ from those of your parents or even the culture in which you were raised. When you look at each valuable, you may select several that belong more on your parents' list than your own.

Define Your Valuables

To identify your valuables, follow these steps:

1. Start with the left-hand column. Read through the list of daily living valuables.
2. Are any of your daily living valuables missing? There is room at the bottom to add what you need.
3. Place a check mark by the ten valuables that are most important to you.

4. Of the ten you selected, circle the five valuables that are most crucial to you. *Remember,* you can have more than five; no one is going to make you give the other ones up, but this is to help you prioritize.

5. Of the five remaining valuables, select the one that is least important to you, the one you could live without, and write that valuable on line 5.

6. Of the four remaining valuables, choose the one you could most easily live without and write it on line 4.

7. Continue eliminating valuables you could live without until you reach the most important valuable. Write that one on line 1.

8. Repeat the process with the destination valuables.

Daily Living Valuables

Truth-seeking	Service
Love	Beauty
Honesty	Honor
Adventure	Intimacy
Justice	Passion
Authenticity	Reason
Intelligence	Compassion
Humility	Cheerfulness
Loyalty	Respect
Spirituality	Courage
Commitment	Elegance
Discipline	Determination
Flexibility	Confidence
Irony	Comfort
Health	Integrity
Creativity	Longevity
Vitality	Growth
Warmth	Comedy
Cheerfulness	Irreverence
Athleticism	Team membership
Fun	Gratitude
Cooperation	Grace
Neatness	Conformity
Cleanliness	_____
Sincerity	_____
Certainty	_____
Assurance	_____

Destination Valuables

Security	Ecstasy
Success	Power
Equality	Salvation
Fame	Respect
Grace	Accomplishment
Wealth	Contribution
Vitality	Endurance
Achievement	Legacy
Peace	Safety
Impact	Nature
Bravery	Harmony
Open spaces	Innovation
Triumph	Breakthrough
Mastery	Conformity
Revolution	Sophistication
Self-actualization	Competence
Variety	Inner harmony
Reputation	Location
Helping society	Personal health
Intellectual status	Privacy
Religion	Wisdom
Power	Self-respect
Authority	_____
Recognition	_____
Truth	_____
Contentment	_____
Freedom	_____

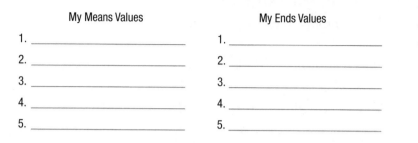

My Means Values	My Ends Values
1. _____	1. _____
2. _____	2. _____
3. _____	3. _____
4. _____	4. _____
5. _____	5. _____

Now that you have identified both your daily living and destination valuables, it is time to compare the lists and see how compatible they are. In the following section you will look into each of your daily living and destination valuables and see whether they work together or in opposition. You don't want to have a destination that ultimately cannot be achieved because your daily living valuables make it too painful to get there. Looking at both now should help you avoid that trap.

We have found many people who realize that their chosen daily living valuables make it hard to achieve their destination valuables. These include people who value certainty at the expense of discovery, people who value religious doctrine at the risk of oppression, people who value freedom at the expense of security for their family. [The choices we make each and every day are governed by our daily living valuables. The choices we make every day add up over time to the destination valuables we are able to achieve.]

The following exercise will help you get a clear sense of which valuables are most important to you in your life and how well your daily living valuables and your destination valuables work together.

Cherish Your Valuables

Write your number one daily living valuable here:

_____

Think through the following questions:

How do you know this is important to you? (For example, what happens to you when it is missing versus when it is present?)

What/who will support this valuable in your life?

What, if any, is the cost to you of not being aligned with this valuable?

What ends can and cannot be achieved through living this valuable consistently?

Finally, does living with this valuable prevent you from achieving your destination valuables?

Protect Your Valuables

What/who works against this valuable in your life?

How can you change the situation?

What will you start doing that will have you more aligned with this valuable over the next week?

Cherish Your Valuables

Write your number one destination valuable here:

_____

Think through the following questions:

How do you know this is important to you? (For example, what happens to you when it is missing versus when it is present?)

What/who will support this valuable in your life?

What, if any, is the cost to you of not being aligned with this valuable?

Finally, is living in pursuit of this destination valuable incongruent with any of your daily living valuables?

Protect Your Valuables

What/who works against this valuable in your life?

How can you change the situation?

What will you start doing that will have you more aligned with this valuable over the next week?

Now that you have completed the Valuables exercise, we ask you to respond to one more question. The only answers that are appropriate are yes or no!

Do your daily living valuables work in concert to help you achieve your destination valuables?

If you are like so many of us, the answer is no. This answer is not something to be too concerned about at this moment in time. We have found that more often than not, when our daily living valuables and our destination valuables are not in total agreement, it is because we have accumulated some valuables from our past that we may want to dump. The following section is designed to help you see if you are in possession of some valuables you may not need or want anymore.

Valuables and Our Environment

Without thinking too hard, write down five things that were valuables in your family or during your childhood (from school, friends, community):

1. _____

2. _____

3. _____

4. _____

5. _____

Which one or two of these do you feel are part of you that you have carried forward or want to carry forward in your life?

_____

_____

_____

Did you reject any of the valuables out of hand? Do any of these valuables make you uncomfortable? Write down any valuables from your family or upbringing that you would not like to carry forward:

_____

_____

_____

As much as we would like to think differently, our environment exerts a great influence on our valuables. As we stated earlier, when adults reach about age thirty-five, they often realize that they are free at last to live their lives the way they want to, not necessarily the way their parents or others wish. Part of the joy of working with people and their valuables is that we have the privilege of helping people create a compelling new set of rules for themselves. In addition to releasing people from valuables that no longer have meaning, we have also found that this can remove the burdens imposed by media and culture.

 ## Snapshot:

Melanie is director of investor relations at one of the world's largest food service companies. She is competent, well liked, and respected; by anyone's standards, she is ex-

traordinarily successful. Before Melanie went back to school for her MBA, she made a living as a catalog model. She openly admits that she is concerned about how she looks. She laughs when she talks about it, but she doesn't agonize about it any longer. She is at home in her admittedly imperfect body, and she tries to get her friends to stop worrying about their jean size. She recently shared this insight:

"About a year ago, it struck me that I don't look at myself critically anymore. I check to make sure everything matches and that my skirt isn't tucked into the back of my pantyhose, you know"—she laughs—"I cover the basics. But I simply don't look at myself and wish I were different anymore. I thought maybe it was the great gift of being over forty. Then I made a very significant connection."

For the first five years of my kids' lives, I had a wonderful nanny. When the kids were napping, she had downtime and would read women's fashion or beauty magazines. There was always a pile of them around, all of which I read when I was younger and stopped buying for myself when I simply ran out of time for that kind of thing. I found myself leafing through her magazines in short moments, you know—waiting for the toast to toast, the water to boil, the child to locate the backpack."

Anyway, she went off to another job when my youngest entered kindergarten, and with her went the magazines. After this, I noticed a big shift in my self-image. I believe that my constant self-criticism was directly connected to the values expressed in those magazines. I have always depended on looking good; I know it has helped me in business. But I realized that, although it's important to me, it just isn't that important. It has its place, but it isn't in my top five anymore. I realized my standards are different than the ones held in advertising; they're more realistic for my life."

I have a new boundary now too: I don't watch prime-time TV, and I don't ever read women's magazines. The minute I do, I start comparing myself and coming up short, which is a total bore and such a waste of time. I can't tell you what a difference it makes in my quality of life.

"Last month we went on vacation, and I put on a bathing suit with no *thought to how I looked and enjoyed frolicking in the waves with my kids. I don't know if you can understand what that means to a former model. It's big. It was a real aha for me, knowing I need to protect myself from the influence of fashion culture. Now I need to figure out how to best help my kids and husband discover and protect what's important to them."*

There are some things that are truly important to us at our core, and there are others that matter because they are important to our culture, our family, our company, our spouse, or our community. Distinguishing between the two can be tricky, and doing so requires a fair amount of attention. It is all too easy to convince ourselves that the valuables that are important to our culture or to those we love must therefore be of equal importance to us. *When relationships begin to wane or to go sour, it is often because of an intense valuables mismatch.*

In our youth, we feel that we have so much time before us that staying focused on what is most important is not a priority. As we age and life picks up speed and responsibilities, and we see time starting to run out, we want to discard those things that are not essential and to focus on the key things. As kids, we can afford to say yes to anything. Only later, when we reap the consequences of barely considered choices, do we start realizing we had better use our time wisely. In midlife many people start feeling the pull to clarify what is most important to them.

■ VALUABLES AND VOCATION ■

Individuals have more choices now than ever before. Bright and talented college kids who are motivated can choose just about any career and make a go of it. Unfortunately, many kids have difficulty making good choices about their careers when they are young. In our experience most people don't even begin to get clear about what is most important to them until they are well into their midthirties. However, the lucky ones have clear and strong preferences early in life.

Snapshot:

Claire turns away from her sleeping mother in her hospital bed and smiles at the nurse, Kimberly, whose name is cheerfully proclaimed by a large tag with a happy face on it. Kimberly, who is hovering at an IV stand, has an air of competence and certainty that seems inconsistent with her youth. Claire knew she was getting older when cops started to look young, but this is truly unusual.

"You must get tired of having to deal with so much technology," Claire says to Kimberly.

"Yeah, it can get to be a drag, but when it all works, it really does make some things easier."

In the week that Claire has been with her mom in the hospital, she has seen the nurses being trained on a new computer system that will decrease dosage errors. It was obvious that the learning curve was frustrating everyone, causing a dip in efficiency.

Kimberly went on, "I became a nurse because I wanted to take care of people, but since I happen to be the computer geek around here, they'll all just freak out if I ever leave." She laughs. "What's important to me is taking care of the patients, and if the technology helps me to do that better, that's great." Motioning with her head at the rogue IV stand, "I'll have to get another one; that's three that have crashed today." Kimberly continues to fuss with the controls and the incessant beeping suddenly stops. "Ah. Okay. That should be good for now. Let me know if it starts up again."

"How long have you been a nurse? You look too young to even be out of college."

"You know, I get that a lot." She laughs. "I look younger than I am, but I'm twenty-two. I finished high school and college in four years, total. My whole life I wanted to be a nurse. My mom is a nurse; my aunt is a nurse. I

used to help them when I was little. It's all I ever wanted." She smiles. Claire thinks she has never met a happier person in her entire life, and that's saying something when it refers to a nurse at the end of an ICU shift.

"How did you know for sure?" Claire asks.

Kimberly is headed for the door. "Just always did." She turns and leans against the wall. "I used to bring home strays and wounded birds and nurse them. It's just what I am. I feel lucky that way." Kimberly turns to go. "I'll be back in a little while to check on your mom." Her sweet smile seems to linger in the doorway as she leaves Claire to marvel at how anyone so young can be so definite about what is important to her.

It is extraordinary to know your deepest desire and then to have the intelligence, gifts, and educational opportunities to support it. How lucky can you get? Kimberly was sure very early on. The rest of us have to feel it out, test the world, and often learn what is important by eliminating little by little what isn't. It's not a crime not to know.

The flip side of Kimberly's extraordinary story is Nat's. Madeleine met Nat at a party a couple of years ago. He was forty-four years old and a high-level editor at an international financial newspaper. When Madeleine met him, his mother had died a year before, and he related that the experience of watching what the nurses did so inspired him that he decided to attend nursing school. At the time Madeleine met him, Nat was three months away from leaving the newspaper, graduating from nursing school, and embarking on an entirely new career.

Both Nat and Kimberly are living lives driven by what is most valuable to them, though they arrived there along radically different paths.

■ NEEDS AND VALUABLES ■

Valuables are the foundation on which we build entire lives. They determine how we choose to see and use our gifts; they dictate our standards; they form the way we draw boundaries. If you are uncertain about what is most important to you, you might be building your house on a foundation that will crumble during the first big rain. In the previous chapter we addressed the basic needs that must be met for you to function optimally. The reason we work with needs first is to help you distinguish between what you *need* and what you *want,* often an extremely fine distinction for many of us.

Needs drive us. Valuables are similar in that they develop whether we want them to or not. Even if you have never heard of valuables as a concept, they shape the way you do things, how you would like others to do things, and the destinations you set out for. To a large degree, needs are not optional—they are a function of our personality and the sum total of who we have become over time. Valuables are also a part of the fabric of who we are, but when it comes to valuables we have more choices. We may not be able to choose our needs, but we can choose to honor our valuables.

How do your Prime Objective, your needs, and your valuables all work together? Right about now it probably feels like a mosh pit to you, which is natural. Let's meet Eric and see how they add up to something useful for him.

 Snapshot:

Eric's father spent his entire working life in the automotive industry as a front line manager. He lived in the hope that someday he could retire on the west coast of Florida, fishing full time. Every weekend was great because he "wasn't at the plant." Everything good in his life was defined as anything that

wasn't work. Eric's dad never made it to Florida; he died of a heart at-tack forty-one days after retiring. Eric decided early on that living a life looking to the future was not for him; he was going to get the most out of every single day.

Our story catches up with Eric twenty years later, just as he is begin-ning to coast a little in a great job as senior director of a successful overnight shipping company. Eric has been with the company from start-up to struggling firm to going public to finally becoming the market leader. He is proud of the firm, proud of his contribution to those innovations that gave the company a jump-start. Eric is most proud of the fact that he has grown with the company and is considered a valuable leader. Recently, however, work has been tough; sales have flattened, and he has been asked to lay off people in order to ensure his unit's profitability. As a result of this unexpected stress, Eric's hair has started to fall out, he breaks out in hives, and for the first time in his life he's having trouble sleeping.

He keeps telling his wife that the layoffs were wrong, wrong, wrong, but he can't seem to come up with a better way of increasing prof-itability. Eric has worked with an executive coach on and off for several years. He remembers that his coach always said, "If you ever want to just have a conversation, if something comes up, feel free to call." Well, Eric thinks, this is definitely something. He sets up an emergency con-versation.

After Eric lays out the situation, he hears his coach clearing his throat.

"That's tough stuff, Eric. Here's the deal. You have a strong need for action, right? Do you think that might be driving you right now?"

Eric took a moment to mull that over. "Well, yeah. It just seems so lame to go along and do the accepted thing. It feels like I'm going down without a fight."

"That sounds right. So tell me a little bit about your Prime Objective at the present moment. I assume you aren't aiming to keep your head down and coast gently to retirement?"

"Are you right about that! In fact, I was just discussing that with my wife. My objective right now is to protect the legacy of this incredible organization we've built."

"All right," said the coach, "so you know you have a need to jump into action, and your Prime Objective is to protect the company's legacy. That's clear. It also seems to me that what is really causing trouble here is your valuables. As I recall, you have very strong valuables around five important things: innovation, reason, intelligence, loyalty, and courage. Let me just check in with you . . . do these still ring true for you?"

"Hmm, let's see—innovation, reason and intelligence, loyalty and courage. Yes, I would say those things are important to me."

"All right, well, that might explain in a nutshell why this situation is driving you nuts. You must feel that with enough good thinking there's got to be a better way, right?"

"That's exactly right," says Eric, feeling relief at seeing things laid out that way and in knowing someone else sees it as well.

His coach continues, "A couple of other things that I remember made an impression on me about you: you work because you love your work, not so you can ride off into the sunset in a golf cart, correct?"

"Well, I'd like to play more golf. It's true that I love my job, and I love this company. I'll probably take a break from the day-to-day craziness; move into a mentoring role or something, eventually. Then I'd like to use my knowledge and experience to contribute to some other businesses. Maybe sit on a few boards."

"That's what I remember. Let's face it, you've helped the company achieve double-digit growth year after year through innovation and the creation of strong relationships with clients. You may not have thought about valuables for a while, you've just been living them. Your valuables are innovation, reason, intelligence, loyalty, and courage. You might think that laying people off violates your valuable of loyalty, which is of course true. But there's more here than loyalty to consider. How do your other valu-

ables come into play here? How can you use them to approach this situation differently?"

Eric was already on his feet, pouncing into action.

"Okay, I've got an idea. I'll call you back," and he was off and running down the hall.

Reason and courage were the valuables that struck him anew. What has been bothering him most about the layoffs is the lack of logic behind them. Eric knows all too well that when you cut workers to reduce costs, you are already in trouble. He also knows that while the effect of reducing the workforce is devastating enough in the short term, it can also kill the future. Eric decided then and there that he needed to get his team together to find a new, more positive approach to improving their profitability, as they had years ago when the adoption of the fax machine cut their business in half overnight. He saw in a flash that they needed to reinvent the business right now rather than go through layoffs and face the difficultly of engaging the remaining employees in picking up the slack.

Eric knows his intelligence and reason will serve him. He also knows that the critical ingredient from a valuables perspective is his courage. He has never had a problem speaking up in the face of overwhelming opposition. He has already earned a reputation as a valuable contributor who is a contrarian only when it really matters.

Eric calls some of his longtime work buddies together, along with some of the sharp new minds, and discusses what he is thinking. They are all dumbstruck with Eric and also pleased because they have also had trouble sleeping lately. The following week, Eric and a select few meet with their former colleague, now CEO, to share different approaches to handling the company's troubles. The CEO admits he is under tremendous pressure. Nevertheless, they have his full attention, and he is still able to listen. Over the next few weeks, the senior leaders meet for hours on end and decide on a new course for the business.

"We are still not sure it will work. But taking this approach will engage everyone in a new way. Being demoralized and depressed sure wasn't

working," Eric tells his coach two months later. "We've all worked too hard to let this thing go the obvious route. Our competition is resorting to lay-offs in order to cut costs. I continue to believe that it causes more harm than good. I thought that at the very least we should try some other measures, pulling together as a company to explore other options. The word is getting around, and productivity is going crazy, our people are so relieved that the pink-slip rain won't be falling anytime soon."

Eric sighs deeply. "Thanks for the reminder about my valuables, coach; I remembered who I am, and it galvanized me to take charge."

Cherishing and protecting your valuables can help you live a life that makes more sense, a life you are proud of. When we know what is important to us, we are able to act with clarity, courage, and passion.

The work of this chapter can be challenging and thought-provoking. Fortunately, we do not have to work on our valuables very often. You will find them handy in the next chapter, on standards, which tend to require more oversight. You'll want to keep your valuables with you at all times, though, to help guide you through your complicated days and to help you reach your destination in top condition.

- Valuables are the champagne of life.
- Your valuables are probably different from those of your family, friends, and coworkers. Being aware of the differences will give you more clarity when making major decisions.
- No one will honor your valuables for you. It is up to you. (If not you, then who?)
- If you don't live them now, when will you? (If not now, then when?)

CHAPTER EIGHT

Name and Claim
Your Standards

■ ▼ ■

How do your standards hurt you?

Standards are the behaviors and practices you hold yourself to. They determine what you demand of yourself in any situation. We all have a list of "shoulds" in our heads as long as our arm—ideas of things we *should* do, ways we *should* behave, a code of conduct or a set of manners we believe we *should* be adhering to. The problem is that although we have consciously chosen a few of them, we are pretty wishy-washy about the rest. The ones we are wishy-washy about hound us and weigh us down. Some are left over from a previous stage of life; some we've absorbed from the culture at large; some are forced upon us; some we are vaguely aware of and only marginally committed to. Unless you have intentionally chosen a standard and made sure it fits with your current life, it will exert a subtle pressure that drains your energy.

Unclear standards cause other problems too. They are often at the root of judgments we pass on others and affect relationships accordingly. It is unproductive to pass judgment and to sentence another based on our own standards. Understanding your own standards and those of others in order to reach clear agreements about acceptable behavior will help you to prevent countless clashes.

Snapshot:

It is 10:00 P.M. on December 21, and Margaret is leaning on her coffee table feeling as if she's about to cry. Incredibly bright, with a string of letters after her name on her business card, Margaret stays at least two steps ahead of everyone else, but she doesn't let it show. When you talk to her she makes you feel as if you are the only person on the planet, peering at you with eyes narrowed in concentration, her head cocked. If she were a cat, her ears would be pricked up. She is always impeccably put together, and to top it off she's a natural blond with peerless taste in accessories. People want to hate her but can't because she is genuinely kind.

As a senior-level operations executive for a large health-care provider, Margaret is used to late hours and hard work. She attributes her success and her many promotions at work to the fact that she hasn't married or had children, devoting most of her waking hours to work. She has never questioned her role of chief communications officer for her family, because all of her siblings have kids, and it's universally though wrongly assumed that she has more free time than anyone else.

Every year at holiday time for the past decade, Margaret has mailed a handmade holiday card accompanied by a newsletter to her grandparents and all her other relatives, updating them on her entire family of six siblings.

But now Margaret realizes that to keep to her usual standard for the holiday she will have to give up her sleep between this night and Christmas day. Her company has recently been acquired, and the workload is especially heavy. She hasn't even had time to shop for the personalized holiday gifts that her staff has come to expect. She catches her own *haggard reflection in the window of her living room and realizes that something has got to give.*

Margaret has become a slave to her standards and she doesn't even know it. She hasn't noticed that her old standard for her holiday routine is no longer feasible in her current situation. Often our standards are disproportionately high for our given situation or environment. At other times they are painfully low. How can we keep up? By understanding what standards really are, what they are *not,* and by keeping an eye on how they fluctuate as our lives change. We also need to understand our standards so we can communicate them appropriately to others—sometimes we impose ours on others without realizing it. You have probably experienced this yourself. Remember the last time you felt the weight of someone else's expectations? It is an extremely unpleasant and unproductive experience.

■ WHAT ARE STANDARDS? ■

Standards are simply the behaviors and practices we demand of ourselves. That seems simple enough. What is not so simple is being crystal clear about what they are and making sure we have systems in place to support those we choose. According to the dictionary, a standard is something established by authority, custom, or general consent to serve as a model or example to be followed, attained, or exceeded. This sounds like a heavy load, and it is. So it is crucial that every single one you have for yourself be carefully examined and revised regularly.

Your standards are like the luggage you pack to sustain you on a trip. The idea is to pack as lightly as possible with only what you need. And no matter how much you travel, you still have to come home and repack every once in a while—you don't want to end up carrying a lot of unnecessary stuff. Each standard you choose has weight and exacts a price. You need to know what you are carrying and what the cost is.

You'll want to make sure your standards are based on what is most valuable to you. The only authority that should be deciding what model of behavior you follow is you.

Some examples of standards are:

I do my best within the time frame allotted.
I have at least one hour to myself every day.
I eat healthy food.
I exceed performance expectations at work.
I say thank you sincerely and often.
I am prepared with directions and the itinerary.
I arrive five minutes early.
I keep my promises.
I remember to show my appreciation for feedback.
I don't allow the gas tank in my car to get empty.

What you may notice about these is the unequivocal language. There is no "trying"; a standard is not something you attempt—it is something you do. Period, end of story.

YOUR STANDARDS

All too often people inherit, acquire, or otherwise get stuck with models of behavior that have nothing to do with their own valuables or personal interests. High standards are fine, but make sure you aren't schlepping around someone else's. It causes way too much internal confusion. Think about it—if you are constantly trying to live up to standards that you didn't even choose, you are bound to run short of motivation eventually.

People often connect their standards to morals or ethics, but the only truly useful foundation for them is your own valuables. The word *moral* comes from *moralis* and *ethics* from *ethikos,* the Latin and the Greek words for "customs" and "habit." The Latin word is associated with rules of behavior, whereas the Greek word is derived from habitat, like our habits. Is each and every one of your standards based on some hard-and-fast moral authority? Which one?

The key is to recognize that no standard is inherently "better" or more right than another—it is right for you, right now, or it is not. Holding to a standard takes commitment and energy. If you are asking yourself to behave in ways that do not reflect your own beliefs or what is important to you, you run the risk of hitting the wall sooner or later.

You'll want to determine *your* standards. You may be clear about a few, but chances are there are others that are not nailed down. What you think is a standard may be simply an old habit that no longer serves you. The first step is to identify the standards you currently have and decide what they are based on. For example: what is your standard for returning a phone call? One hour? Twenty-four hours? Three days? When was this standard instituted? Is it yours or your previous boss's? Does it still work for your current life? To what extent are your standards aligned with those of the culture you live or work in? To what extent are they at odds?

Let's take a look at how this plays out for you in your work life. In filling out the grid on page 151, you will need to consider many of the small day-to-day tasks you take for granted. You may be surprised to find that there are gaps between your own standards and the expectations of your work environment. Every small gap will represent a source of low-level tension that you can eliminate.

Consider these questions in the context of your current work setting:

What is the standard in your work environment for:	What is your own?	What is the accepted standard in your work culture?	What is the gap, if any? Is your standard too high or too low?	How does this affect you? How can you change your standard?
Promptness To what extent are you on time and prepared?				
Accuracy To what extent do you review your work for errors?				
Communication Do you share information fully with everyone who needs to know?				
Goal Clarity To what extent are you clear about what you are trying to accomplish with each task?				
One-to-One Meetings To what extent do you provide opportunity for regular check-ins with all team members?				
Returning E-mails and Phone Calls What is your idea of returning messages in a timely fashion?				
Confidentiality To what extent can you be fully trusted not to gossip?				
Meeting Management To what extent are your meetings focused and productive?				
Social Time vs. Focused Work Time Do you use your time as well as you could?				
Deadlines To what extent do you deliver on your promises?				
[Add yours here] _____ _____				

Any news here for you? Are any of your standards too high? Too low? What will you do about it? What standards will you change?

Setting a new standard for yourself is a tricky business and not to be taken lightly. As we've said earlier, when you fail to live up to standards, it'll make you feel lousy. So be extremely picky about the standards you do choose, and once you've done it, set yourself up to win. For example, if you have decided that one of your standards is that you keep your promises, make only promises you are absolutely sure you will be able to keep, barring an act of God. If one of your standards is that you eat healthy food, it makes a lot of sense to put a biweekly trip to the grocery store on the calendar.

We know a president of an insurance organization who had the standard of being home with her kids in the evenings. She also had the standard that she returned every call and e-mail on the same day they were received. As she rose in the organization, the two standards became mutually exclusive, and her stress level became unmanageable. There was no way she could maintain both standards—one of them had to go. One of the biggest favors you can do for yourself is to set only standards you can actually keep.

How do you know if your standards are too low? In the workplace generally people tell you. Even when people aren't direct, they drop clues—like your new manager might complain how irritated he is about a report he just got in which the points weren't well thought through. That is useful information, even it wasn't directed at you.

You are constantly getting feedback. The information you need is at your fingertips. You have to pay attention. Keep your antennae up because feedback is often subtle, and most people will only tell you once. Most people are embarrassed to give feedback more than once. No one wants to nag. Listen carefully to the clues people give you—they are a gift designed to help you modulate your standards to be successful in your environment.

■ STANDARD DECISIONS ■

Once you've given some thought to your current standards, you'll notice how they affect every decision that comes your way. Your standards are reflected in all the decisions you make, large and small. For example, if one of your standards is that you keep one hour of every day free for yourself, it will naturally limit your social engagements. If you can't decide what to say yes to, your standards will be your guide. We know an advertising executive who travels a great deal for work. He has a standard that when he is not traveling, he spends at least half of his evenings at home with his family. He accepts the social engagements that he must and limits the others. Standards, when they are specific, help you to set boundaries.

Do you see how important standards are? To attempt to live up to standards that have been imposed by your work culture or are a holdover from family or old friends is a burden. Life is too short. Make every standard, in your work and in your personal life, yours and *only* yours.

■ KEEP YOUR STANDARDS FOR YOURSELF! ■

Standards are strongly affected by our family, the culture we are raised in, and the culture we work in. Standards are based on what we think is important, and they are often based on things that have become natural to us. A classic example of this is the very obvious and often remarked upon variation in standards about being "on time." In some cultures it is considered terribly rude to arrive after an appointed time, whereas in others it is considered rude to arrive on time. Neither is inherently right or wrong. But this does not keep us from judging others harshly for having a standard different from our own.

Our standards govern almost all judgments we pass on others. Judgment is a natural impulse that can be curbed by understanding the culture and history of others and attempting to assess what is valuable to them. This takes self-awareness, discipline, and self-control. Usually we default to assuming that most people are like us, should be like us, and are somehow faulty if they are not. We refer to this as the BLM (Be Like Me) syndrome.

Let's see how two valuable employees with radically different worldviews and sets of standards cause problems for each other.

Snapshot:

Ruth is tall and dark with a set to her jaw that she defines as Texan. When she is annoyed, which is most of the time, her lips automatically compress into a grim gray line. Stacey is short, blond, and undeniably perky. When she is stressed she never looks annoyed, she simply trembles on the verge of tears. Ruth and Stacey despise each other, and their manager is ready to pull his hair out. He has assigned them to work together for their different and complementary skill sets, both of which are needed for the success of the project. He has given their unpleasant working relationship three months to resolve itself before he fires them both and starts from scratch. He would hate to do that because each of them is talented in her own right, and they are both up to speed on the details of this high-stakes project.

What's the problem? Ruth is the Excel spreadsheet, Access database, report-generating queen; everyone depends on her systematic analytical approach. Ruth gets crazed when people make small errors in spelling, calculations, or the recording of any data. When colleagues call her with questions, she will actually tell them she thinks they're wasting her time with stupid questions. She thinks Stacey is an idiot. Ruth can't figure out how Stacey even got, much less keeps, her job given how many errors she makes. Ruth also can't figure out how any university gave Stacey an advanced degree considering that she can't spell or accurately import information into spreadsheets.

But when colleagues call in with questions, they're relieved when Stacey answers the phone; they know they'll be received warmly and will get a thorough explanation of exactly what they need to know. And they'll get a follow-up call. They also know that Stacey will give them insights that are geared to their own way of doing things. With Ruth they'll barely get a small clue as to their next step, nothing more than a hint of what to do. And they always leave Ruth feeling that their intelligence has been questioned.

Both Ruth and Stacey bring crucial talents to the current project, and neither is as strong alone as they are together. Their manager places Ruth in charge of data gathering and reporting and gives Stacey the responsibility for client-facing communication. Both are insulted by this division of labor.

Stacey and Ruth have been to a training course on personality types, and one thing they agree on (though they've never discussed it) is that the instructor lied when he said that no one personality type is inherently better or more valuable than any other.

Ruth has standards that are based on the valuables she grew up with—her family played word games and held crossword competitions. She and her siblings competed for grades, and her parents, both physicists, used to bring home interesting problems for the family to solve at the dinner table. Accuracy is Ruth's lifeblood—literally her way of connecting to people. Stacey, on the other hand, grew up in a world in which empathy and gauging emotional states were key to the well-being of her mother. She was valued for how well she took care of the people around her. These are two diametrically opposed sets of valuables with two corresponding sets of standards and no middle ground. Without understanding and generosity of spirit, conflict is a foregone conclusion.

We'd all like to think that adults in the workplace do not engage in such insanity, yet it happens every day. When standards and valuables clash, it often leads to the kind of bad behavior you'd expect from a five-year-old. Of all the stuff that drives bosses crazy, this may be the most common, and it is certainly the hardest to impact. We've seen organizations apply training, coaching, employee assistant programs, therapists, and mediation to situations like the one between Ruth and Stacey with minimal success. All we can say is that if you (yes, you) are at loggerheads with someone in your workplace, take a long hard look at how different your valuables and standards are to see if there is a clash.

How do you know when your own standards are getting you into trouble? When you think things like: "Boy, are they stupid," "What an idiot," "Who let them in the door?" When you roll your eyes as someone walks away from you, when you begin avoiding calls. When you stop giving someone the benefit of the doubt, when you begin to seek evidence to support your judgment. You know what we're talking about. We all do it. This isn't a problem because you are being uncharitable, even if that is the case. We aren't asking you to be nicer. We're asking you to be *smarter*.

To broaden your horizon, stop for one minute and ask yourself a series of questions that may provide the whack upside the head we all need sometimes:

> *What makes me get so nuts about this person?*
> *What is it that makes this person so radically different from me?*
> *How does that make them better or worse than me?*
> *According to whom?*
> *What value do they bring that I do not/will not/cannot?*
> *How does it serve me to discount them?*

This may provide you with a fresh perspective that will help you to behave yourself. If there is a true mismatch, you will have to get over yourself and manage your judgment. Your standards are yours and yours alone, and if you seek to impose them on others without their agreement, you will be lonely indeed.

Now—finding a way to appreciate what the other person brings to the table is another thing altogether! And if you access the more generous side of your nature to do this, more power to you. You will certainly be making the best of a difficult situation.

If you are thinking, *Oh my god, you'd have to be so immature to need this advice*, you are a finer human being than the rest of us. You would also be among the minority who have no conflict in their lives. Contrary to popular opinion, it takes only one person to deescalate conflict. Once one party backs down, the other usually ceases their own defensive posturing, backing down too. If you think you are above acting like a child because you can't see past what's important to you, we challenge you to think again. We have never once met a client who hasn't created the dynamic of the BLM syndrome somewhere in their life, causing themselves as well as others a great deal of discomfort. Step away from the BLM syndrome and save yourself a lot of time and energy.

STAYING ON TOP OF STANDARDS

Standards are set on a continuum. Often they are either too high or too low for the situation you are in and need to be adjusted to stay "just right." They must be *monitored* for their appropriateness as your role or surroundings change. A perfect example of this is the shock that straight A high school students experience when they arrive at college. Having been academic stars in high school, they are suddenly surrounded by peers who are as accomplished as they are, if not more so. The bar has been raised; the standard for excellence has shifted. Another key moment when standards need to be raised, often causing trauma, is when an employee is promoted out of a group. The rules change, straining relationships that once felt easy and enjoyable.

It is important to remember that standards are a choice: they must change or shift when they begin to do more harm than good, as what happened with Margaret. Her holiday letter, which started out as fun and rewarding, became oppressive. Margaret was submitting to what she felt was a tradition, with old rules that *she* had made up in the first place. It is up to her to rewrite her own rules. What is so astonishing, but so common, is Margaret's blindness to her own power over the situation.

The example of Margaret may seem absurd to you if communication is not a strong valuable for you, but we'd bet you money that you are currently submitting to some outdated rules of your own that you aren't aware of. There is no great big rule book in the sky that dictates our standards. We decide them for ourselves from the context we are *currently* in. Let's observe what happens when outdated standards become entrenched.

 ## Snapshot:

Dave is forty-nine and feels fifty bearing down on him all too fast. He runs five miles every morning, a holdover from the physical discipline he learned while in the military. The khakis he wears on casual Fridays have been so well ironed they look like they could stand up on their own. His team suspects he puts starch in his underwear. His boss loves him, but his team hates him, and although he's aware of it, he is sick and tired of their whining. Like his dad always used to say: "When the going gets tough, the tough get going."

Dave is getting worried, though. At his last performance review, his boss expressed his appreciation for how much Dave got done and his amazement at how Dave's team, alone of all those in the company, had kept their numbers up. He did point out, however, that Dave had to find a way to stop leaving bodies behind. "The numbers are great," he said, "but the cost of regularly replacing your sales managers is having a negative impact on the business unit as a whole. Dave"—he took a breath, *frowned, and went on—"you've got to find a way to produce without losing so many people. I'd like you to consider working with a coach to review some possibilities for changing your style a little bit."*

Dave was infuriated. What did the company want him to do? Become a soft touch like Pete "the marshmallow" down the hall? He just doesn't understand why people are such namby-pambys these days. When he was a rookie, he worked his butt off. Now he feels these kids want something for nothing. He works late nights and weekends to fix the substandard and sloppy reports prepared by his sales team, and he stews about it. On Monday mornings he calls them on the carpet and tells them how their work is well below par.

What does this cost Dave? He would define his state as alternately frantic, panting for breath, and feeling hostile and trapped. Dave is rapidly burning out. He goes home and rails to his wife, "They want me to produce the numbers, but they don't want to deal with the consequences." Dave's wife, who has seen this train coming from miles away and worries constantly about his stress level, says, "Dave, maybe you could find a way to produce the same numbers without killing yourself or your team. Why don't you take them up on the coach idea; there has to be a better way."

Two weeks later Dave's new coach walks in and hands him the 360-degree feedback report. "Wow," he says, "people really respect you, Dave: your vision, your drive. But you've got to change some of your methods or you're going to be a one-man band."

"Yeah, no kidding."

And the work begins.

First Dave vents, letting off some steam. This allows the coach to understand what is important to Dave: winning, error-free paperwork, hard work for great reward. He also starts to comprehend that Dave's standards are implicit and unclear to his team, who, as shown in his reading of the 360-degree report, often feel ambushed by them. He also knows from experience that the standards Dave holds are needlessly high. He asks

Dave the question "If you were able to let go of your idea of how people should behave and just concentrate on what needs to be done to keep the numbers up, what would be different?"

Dave looks at his coach with his lips pursed in annoyance and while thinking *Who does this guy think he is?* considers the question. There is a long silence.

"Dave, I'm serious. Is your judgment worth the pain you are in right now?" asks the coach.

Dave laughs and says, "The only thing causing my pain is unreasonable quotas."

"That's bull and you know it," shoots back the coach. "You're so close to being the kind of manager who inspires people instead of burning them out. What's it going to take to make the leap?"

Dave stifles a desire to pummel his coach, because he knows that he is right. "Okay. Here's what I'm going to do. My team is exceeding their sales goal; that's a standard they seem to keep up month after month. So I'll try to go easier about some other things. Where do you think I should give in?"

The coach says, "Well, Dave, what are the most important things to you in order of priority?"

Dave takes a minute to make a list of priorities on the legal pad on his desk:

- Exceed goal
- Friday reports in by 3:00 P.M.
- All meetings start on time
- Have clients be surprised by how fast we get proposals to them
- Clients never see a single typo
- Establish and study exactly why we win business and why we lose business
- Team keeps me in the loop, and I know where each account is in the sales cycle

When Dave finishes the list, he looks up at his coach with a "well, isn't that interesting" look on his face.

His coach asks, "What's interesting about your list?"

"I see what is most important and what I should do."

"Okay," Dave says , "it seems to me that the only items here I absolutely need are the ones that contribute to the sales goal. So those would be the numbers of contacts and proposals and the quality of the follow-up. I could redesign the reporting format to reduce its bean-counting aspects. That would make it quicker and easier for the team to complete. I've got to be able to get well-prepared reports without doing the work myself or driving everybody crazy with unreasonable demands. I won't worry about typos on the report, only the content. I won't redo others' work."

Dave's coach breathed a sigh of relief. Old standards can be difficult to break. When Dave speaks to his team about his new standards and warns them that it's going to be hard for him to change, they agree that writing them up on the big whiteboard in the conference room will help everyone remember what the focus is—including Dave.

Three weeks later, Dave arrives home for the weekend at 5:30 P.M., surprising the heck out of his wife.

"Let's go to dinner and catch a movie" he says. "It's been a while."

By using the Three Perspectives as a guide, Dave realized that others saw him as a hard-nosed control freak, an impression that did not enhance his effectiveness. Some of the standards that were designed to make him effective in an earlier part of his life were no longer relevant. Dave had to go back to the drawing board and focus on what mattered most to get the job done. Once he had reformulated his standards, he communicated them to the people who were affected by them. He also asked for support in keeping them clear and not sliding back to his old habits. His team was delighted to comply.

■ CLEAR AGREEMENTS ■

Earlier we talked about not imposing our standards on others. That doesn't mean that when it's important we shouldn't *communicate* them to others. Keep your standards *for* yourself but not *to* yourself. It isn't fair to hold others to standards they aren't aware of and haven't agreed to. *When people have to accomplish something together, they must reach agreements on what the standards are going to be for all concerned.* The higher the stakes are, the greater the clarity in our agreements must be.

The more assumptions we make, the greater the risk of implicit standards being broken. Assumptions are at the root of most misunderstandings. People often ascribe different meanings to the same word—you may think that *finished* means a complete first draft of a document, while your colleague thinks it means the proofed final version. When a group has a lot of members from different time zones, *end of business day* must be clearly defined by a specific time zone. So many meetings happen on the phone these days that many people often forget to designate who calls whom.

Attention to and agreement about the tiny details, like time zones, can make or break a project. An in-depth discussion of standards helps all involved avoid time-consuming and costly mix-ups.

■ CLEAR AGREEMENT AVOIDANCE ■

We always have a good reason for doing what we do, so when we know we must have clear agreements but avoid making them, you can be sure there is a reason for it. Reasons we have heard include:

I don't have the time.
I'm afraid people will think I am too nitpicky, too detail focused.

I'm afraid people will think I don't trust them.
I prefer not to be pinned down myself.

All valid, and all recipes for disaster.

The Time Trap. Time and again we have experienced that putting in the time up front saves time on the back end. The old adage "A stitch in time" is ancient wisdom that has stood the test of the ages.

Fear of Being a Nitpicker. No one wants to be thought of as anal or compulsive, but those that don't have the patience to engage in the detailed ground-laying are often begrudgingly grateful to those who press for clarity.

Trust Now, Pay Later. The issue of trust is extremely delicate, and cultural differences can complicate things even further. It is important to remember that trust is built on respect over time. You can approach others with your desire for clear agreements with the utmost respect by simply telling the truth; something along the lines of "It is my experience that these things can get complicated. Would you mind if we set some ground rules so everyone knows where they stand?" or "Since we aren't that familiar with one another, it would be helpful for me to get a clear picture of how you work best" should help do the trick.

Commitment Phobia. The last reason is extremely common and insidious. Many people prefer to keep things loose so that they can slide by on quality expectations or deadlines if time gets tight. If you think this applies to you, and you know who you are, you are probably someone who juggles a lot and is proud of how much you get done. Or you may be trying to fly under the radar, knowing you are getting by with substandard work. Either way, you are just waiting to get caught with your standards down, and this causes significant if imperceptible stress. *You* know when you are trying to get away with something, and when you admit it to yourself, it feels terrible. When you come clean about this, it can eliminate a huge energy drain. The relief is worth whatever freedom you feel you have to give up.

Clear agreements help everyone know up front what you can expect of others and what they can expect of you. The very simple worksheet has been used by hundreds of our clients. Using it will help you set your standards from the beginning.

As you reviewed the worksheet did you notice places where you are not in line with your colleagues' standards? Do you see some spots where perhaps your standards are too high for the situation? Too low? Where is there a lack of clarity the with the people you are working with? What conversations must take place to make sure that everything is as clear as can be?

We promised earlier that we would provide you with an exercise to make sure that each of your standards is based on what matters most to you. The exercise will also help you use your standards to make decisions that support you in your quest toward your Prime Objective. Finally, it will help you design a plan to communicate effectively about your standards.

Standards Exercise

Part 1. **Connect your valuables to standards**

In the chapter on valuables you identified both daily living and destination valuables. Place those in the left-hand column of the chart below and then define a standard that will support that valuable. Standards can be represented by a habit, a regular practice, or a commitment.

The Clear Agreements Worksheet

What?	What are we trying to accomplish? What is the scope? What does *finished* mean? What are the significant milestones? What will it cover? What is left out? What are we *not* doing?
Why?	Whom will it serve? What is the fundamental purpose? Whom will it affect most if we succeed? If we fail?
When?	When do we start? What is the final deadline? What are the milestone deadlines? What are the consequences of a missed deadline?
Where?	Exactly what physical location will be used? What time zone will be the standard? Whose equipment, phones, cars? Where do expenses get assigned?
Who?	Who will be responsible for what? Whom do we report to? Who needs to be consulted? Who needs to keep informed? Who will meet with whom and how often? Who will follow up with whom? Who will be left holding the bag?
How?	What will our processes be? How do decisions get made? How do we express disagreement? How will we know we are on track? What language will we use? What common behaviors do we agree on? What do we expect in terms of quality? How quickly do we agree to return phone calls and e-mails? How late is okay? What standards of excellence do we take for granted? How will we know we are successful? What constitutes failure?

Valuable	Standard
Grace	Pray ten minutes every day. Thank at least one person per day.
Elegance	Clothes match, are spotless, clean, and pressed. No clutter in my personal space.
Alacrity	Done is better than perfect—deadlines are sacrosanct. Say no when/if I can't do the job.

Valuable Write yours here:	Standard What standards might support this valuable?

Part 2. **Consider and adjust your standards**

What standards do you have that you cannot connect with a valuable?

1. _____

2. _____

3. _____

4. _____

Consider these questions before you decide on keeping this standard for yourself:

➠ What is the cost of this standard to you and your coworkers/family/spouse/friends/pets?

➠ What need is being met by behaving this way?

➠ What or whose standard are you trying to live up to?

➠ What would your life be like if you did not have to keep this standard?

➠ Where did this standard come from?

➠ Whose is it really? Is it really yours?

➠ How does it serve you/contribute to your quality of life?

➠ How might you raise/lower this standard to better suit the realities of your life?

➠ What might you change about this standard that would release and delight you?

Write the chosen or reshaped standards here:

1. _____

2. _____

3. _____

4. _____

What standard are you willing to ditch?

Part 3. **Communicate your standards**

Remember that there will be individuals who do not agree with and will not support you in lowering or raising a standard. The more you do to help others understand your standard, and the reasons for it, the better. You will need to draw boundaries with people who cannot or will not help you.

Who needs to know about your new standards? Write the chosen or reshaped standards here:

1. _____

Who needs to know? How can you tell them in a way that will help them to understand and be willing to help you?

2. _____

Who needs to know? How can you tell them in a way that will help them to understand and be willing to help you?

3. _____

Who needs to know? How can you tell them in a way that will help them to understand and be willing to help you?

4. _____

Who needs to know? How can you tell them in a way that will help them to understand and be willing to help you?

- Standards are intimately connected to your valuables. Know your valuables first, and your standards will become clear.
- Figure out when you are a slave to your standards, and set yourself free.
- Reset your standards as your circumstances and surroundings change.
- Be careful of the way you judge others based on your own standards.
- Agree on shared standards when working with others to avoid conflict.

CHAPTER NINE

Draw and Defend
Your Boundaries

*How did you let yourself
become a doormat?*

boundary is a line in the sand. It is what we allow others to do to or around us. It is essentially the permission we grant people in our environment to do certain things. When someone has overrun a boundary they have gone "beyond the pale." *Pale* in this context comes from the Latin *palus,* which is defined as "a boundary marker driven into the ground to fence off territory." In this case we are talking about your emotional territory. Boundaries, like needs, are deeply personal. And like needs, we often feel nervous about having them. Because we know that once we state them, we'll have to defend them. In all of us there is the dim memory of the child on the playground who says, "Hey, cut it out," only to hear the dreaded response "Oh yeah? Who's gonna make me?" That's right—if you are going to have boundaries, you have to be ready to enforce them.

But first you have to know what they are. Understanding, articulating, and enforcing your boundaries is important because breaches cause tiny drains on your energy and focus. The drain may be almost imperceptible, but the effects add up over time and cause sudden defensive blowups that can feel like bolts out of the blue. Just as you need to make a choice to get your needs met responsibly, you must do the same in drawing and defending your boundaries to maintain the strength you need to be at your best.

Snapshot:

David is everyone's best friend. Sharp as a tack, it surprised no one when he sailed through one of the world's best business schools and immediately went to work for a top management-consulting firm. David rose quickly through the ranks; his work ethic is the stuff of legend. His friends joke about his cell phone addiction, and when his kids were little, they thought Daddy's phone headset was a part of his anatomy.

David travels the world on business, mentors new associates, runs his business school alumni group, is president of his coop board, and recently joined the board of a private school he hopes his daughter will attend. His reputation as someone who always goes the extra mile encourages people to leave him messages that begin, "I hate to ask, but you're the only one I can trust with this." Recently David has begun feeling anxious every time he checks his voice mail because he knows there will be more requests that will intrigue, excite, and engage him.

David is also known throughout the company as being the role model for outstanding client relations. But when his already truncated night of sleep in Hong Kong was interrupted at 5:00 A.M. by a call from a client who angrily screamed himself into a fury over an alleged mistake made by an associate, David started to wonder how things had come to this.

During the long flight home, he admits to an older colleague who has been a mentor to him that he often feels like a piece of meat hanging over a pool of piranhas. When his friend hums "I'm Just a Girl Who Can't Say No," from the musical Oklahoma, David laughs—but he also knows it is time for a change.

oundaries set limits. The military calls them "no fly zones," and they mean Keep Out! Well-defined and maintained boundaries work in exactly the same way. You might possibly feel that setting and enforcing boundaries is presumptuous or pushy. After all, *"Who do you think you are?"* Who has not felt the sting of that question? It is designed to make you wonder, Who *do* I think I am? Who do I think I am to say no? Who am I to impose my will on others? Who am I to take up space? Who am I, in other words, to claim rights and set boundaries?

We think it's a good idea to ask, "Who do you think you are?" so that the next time it floats across your mind you'll have an answer. And in the context of boundaries, the answer is: I am someone who draws the line, gently but firmly.

What would you say if we proposed that you are 100 percent responsible for the way you are treated and 100 percent responsible for what people expect of you? We will challenge you to evaluate every single relationship you have in light of what aspects of it you have chosen and those you did not choose. This includes your relationship with yourself.

Your evaluation may reveal that some of the people you have relationships with regularly exhibit behaviors that drive you to distraction. Then you can choose to try to impact those behaviors or not. You can explain the situation and formulate clear and concise requests of others and test their willingness and ability to honor those requests. They may think you are unreasonable—perhaps you are. If we were all reasonable, all relationships would be simpler. But at least you will have opened a dialogue, and you can assess the degree to which you can or cannot exert control over aspects *not* chosen by you.

Having boundaries, like every other Leverage Point in this book, is about becoming crystal clear about how you intend your life, job, and relationships to be and then making *choices* based on those intentions. We don't mean to imply that you'll always have full control, but you may have more than you think. It is our experience that you have a lot more control over how you experience your relationships than you are willing to admit. There is only one way to find out. This is where the work you've done on getting your needs met really pays off. After you understand what you need, it is much easier to draw the line.

▪ SAYING NO ▪

David may have laughed at the tune, but he realized he did need to learn to say no. His first response to just about everything was yes. He sees himself as a yes kind of guy—a can-do, charge-ahead, positive-attitude person. David's habit of saying yes is first a product of how he sees himself and his enormous amount of energy. His ability to live up to his self-image has trained the people around him to see him the same way. Now he has a reputation to maintain. And a vicious circle has been created—a perfect product of what was originally a good thing. It is not that David is surrounded by grasping people who are out to take advantage of him. It is that David's capacity to live up to his self-image has finally hit its limits, and it's time to surrender to reality.

Most of us have a lot less energy than David, and when we find ourselves in the position of having overpromised, we are forced to renege. For those with a need to accomplish or a valuable of service, this can be a colossal but subtle drain on energy. So the first person we need to draw boundaries with is ourselves.

The foundation of the drive to acquiesce to requests that we know will strain our resources is almost always an unmet need. The need to please others and be well regarded is a common one. But there are others, like a need to achieve; a need to be involved and to make an impact might also be a factor. Another is the need to satisfy curiosity; we saw with David that each new request sparked his interest, even though he knew it might drain him even further.

As we stated earlier, having a clear grasp of what your needs are can provide tremendous support to helping you understand what your boundaries need to be. Once you know what you can and cannot say yes to, you can apply the concept to improving your relationships.

▪ BOUNDARIES AND RELATIONSHIPS ▪

In relationships it might seem easier initially to let things roll off your back, letting yourself be the victim, letting someone else be "impossible" or "the bad guy." You can convince yourself that you are easygoing and that you can take it, whatever "it" is. The long-term cost of such rationalizations, however, is huge. Consider the last time you blew up at someone inappropriately, in a way that was out of proportion to the event. Did that person cross a boundary you hadn't articulated or that you didn't even know you had? Has this ever happened to you? Did you have the time to stop and think about it? Did you just assume the other person was to blame and go along your way? Think back to the last time someone did or said something you couldn't stand and you thought any of the following:

What were they thinking?
How could they do/say that?
Don't I do enough around here?
What terrible manners!
How could they not know that?
What planet are they from?

Or did you stop to ask yourself: *Hmmm. How did I contribute to this event? What might I have done to prevent it? How could they have known that that would send me through the roof?* When a relationship has a difficult moment, it is much easier to assume that the other is at fault than it is to admit that we might have had a hand in creating the situation.

We said that we would challenge you to examine every important relationship you have. One of the things that people remark on when they begin work with a coach is that their relationships either radically improve or they disappear. That is exciting but potentially scary. Remember what we said earlier about choice. Look at each of your relationships and choose whether you are going to do one of three things:

1. Invest in improving it significantly so that the satisfaction of both parties is deeply increased
2. Decide that it is wonderful just as is
3. Develop a plan to divest yourself of the relationship because it is not worth the tremendous effort it takes to maintain it. You may, upon reflection, realize that a relationship that was once productive now offers diminishing returns.

We are not suggesting that you must jettison every difficult relationship you have. That would be absurd. In some cases you can discuss what matters most to you and even slightly improve the relationship. If you decide to maintain a relationship even though it is tremendously difficult and has a negative impact on your well-being, that is a *choice* you make. This kind of choice is usually based on a strong need to fulfill duty or having loyalty as a valuable. If this is the case, however, when you feel drained by someone whom you have chosen to sustain a relationship with, you can remind yourself that you have made a choice and that you are not a victim.

Why is this crucial? Because when we do not feel "at choice" in a relationship, especially with someone who does not respect our boundaries, we become a victim. Feeling like a victim breeds resentment, which is a bitter and insidious emotion. It creeps in quietly on stocking feet and sets up permanent residence before we've even noticed it. And then it feeds itself; it seeks evidence to justify its existence, and it nurses itself to gain strength. Resentment kills everything good in its path: respect, affection, and trust. Resentment can also destroy that which makes life most worth living: joy, passion, and pleasure. And resentment hurts no one so much as the bearer. The author Anne Lammott, whose characters often struggle to be better people, wrote in *Crooked Little Heart*: "Harboring resentment is like taking rat poison and waiting for the rat to die."

If you are waiting for the proverbial rat to die, there is a good chance that you have a relationship rife with resentment, a fairly good sign that some boundaries have been overrun. Choosing not to set and enforce boundaries is a serious mistake. It is harmful to your relationships and a potential personal catastrophe waiting to happen. Let's take a look at how this can play itself out.

Snapshot:

Brian is crazy about the consultant who has come in to help him run a new high-profile project. Suzanne is smart, funny, thorough, and was initially a bit of a puzzle to Brian. He couldn't quite figure how someone so young could have been a VP at her old company and how, in her early thirties, she could afford to work solely on a project-by-project basis, taking six months of the year to paint on Martha's Vineyard. However, once Brian experienced her no-nonsense meetings and take-no-prisoners efficiency, it all made sense. Brian realizes he is the lucky winner in the project worker sweepstakes, because Suzanne is extremely competent, always thinking things through and coming up with action plans that include contingency backups on all their main points. He is relieved and grateful because when the project ended up in his lap, he could not see how it was going to get done; his schedule was already overbooked.

One Friday after a long week the entire project crew is eating in their cubicles, working away through the lunch break so they can leave the office at a reasonable hour. Then Brian walks in, obviously exasperated from his morning meetings and already late for the next one. He gazes around at his entire staff for a long moment and then barks, "No more food up here! From now on everybody eats in the cafeteria. This is disgusting!" He walks into his office and uncharacteristically slams the door shut behind him.

His staff all stand up in their cubicles and look at one another, perturbed, embarrassed, and mystified. Why would the usually reasonable Brian act like such an autocratic jerk?

What set this scene in motion? Had the project been derailed? And where is Suzanne? What will Ms. Perfect think of the new edict? Suzanne, like everyone else, goes to the cafeteria and brings lunch back to her desk. But Brian isn't the only one who has noticed that Suzanne eats healthy foods like salmon, broccoli, Brussels sprouts, and once an especially pungent seaweed soup, all of which happen to make Brian gag. Since childhood Brian has been sensitive about food smells, but he hates admitting it to anyone because it seems so petty. Brian has been aware of the fish and other smells for a couple of weeks, but he was just too thrilled with Suzanne to say anything. And he was afraid that she might take it personally, possibly cutting back on her performance. So he let things slide while his frustration built until on one really bad day at the end of a long and difficult week, the boundary no one knew about was violated yet again and he exploded.

How hard would it have been for Brian to say the following? "Suzanne, you may think it's peculiar—my wife sure does—but I can't tolerate strong food smells. Would you mind terribly staying down in the cafeteria when you choose cooked foods rather than a sandwich?"

Suzanne might have found it inconvenient to eat in the cafeteria, but wouldn't that be preferable to everyone on the team thinking Brian is a psycho boss? Which is better: my boss is a bit peculiar about food, or my boss is a psycho? All it takes for a well-respected guy like Brian to develop a bad reputation is one unreasonable outburst. Unfortunately, all the months of even-tempered good behavior count for almost nothing. No one in a leadership position can afford out-of-character behavior—it might be forgiven, but the damage to the trust that takes so long to build is huge.

Brian got caught with his boundaries down. Everyone does sometimes, even those who think of themselves as tough, direct people. No one *wants* to get caught in a situation that causes them to behave in a way that is inconsistent with their self-image or that they know will cost them trust or respect. *No one* comes to work planning to act like a big jerk. When we do behave really badly, often no one is more surprised than ourselves, and it always happens when we are already stressed and a boundary no one knew was there is crossed. So protect yourself in advance. Know and articulate your boundaries in anticipation of stress. Prepare for stress—it is one of the few things you can count on.

▪ WHY DON'T WE SET BOUNDARIES? ▪

1. **Boundaries change.** It can be hard to keep up.

   Just like standards, boundaries change as we change, and sometimes we neglect to reclarify and rearticulate them for ourselves. It can be hard to recognize when a boundary changes. We grow and change at an imperceptibly slow rate, and considering all the distractions of daily life, we can easily miss our own transformation. A classic redefinition of our boundaries often emerges when we get a promotion. One of the hardest things to navigate is remaining friends with those who were once coworkers and now are underlings. While everyone wants to remain friends, the fact that one person is now senior causes a necessary shifting of all parties' boundaries. Suddenly it is inappropriate to share certain personal information or for direct reports to reveal more than is absolutely necessary.

2. **We are afraid of what people will think.** There is always someone we don't want to annoy or hurt.

This point is deeply connected with the Three Perspectives. In Brian's case he wanted to be seen as easygoing and normal; he wanted others to see him that way too. Brian saw his aversion to food smells as odd and was afraid others would interpret it the same way. Brian was embarrassed by his sensitivity but not nearly as embarrassed as he was about the way he lashed out.

Sometimes, due to cultural mores or our perception of hierarchy, we actually feel that we are not allowed to have boundaries. This issue is not limited to the administrative assistant putting up with off-color remarks from her boss; it also shows up in relationships with spouses, siblings, and friends. Often we fail to draw a boundary because we fear that if we do, it will put the whole relationship into question or jeopardy. In Brian's case, although he had rank, he was nervous about the possibility of decreasing Suzanne's effectiveness.

We are all afraid of being judged, but you will be judged no matter what you do. Not setting boundaries because you fear what people will think of you will always end up hurting you as well as the people around you. Setting your boundaries up front, training and expecting people to behave in ways that support your best self, will lead them to forget the past, remembering only your best self. You may get teased at first, but so what? Generally people only tease those they like.

3. **We lack the language to express boundaries effectively.**

Even if we know we have boundaries, we often lack the appropriate skills to put them into words. The language of Western culture has a limited vocabulary of assertiveness, and it is most often perceived as bossy, dominating, or demanding. When we want someone to stop doing something, we are limited to no, stop, and don't. Instead, the language needed to set boundaries must point out in a neutral way the action that needs to be stopped or taken. It also must offer an alternative if possible, giving people permission to say no.

One way to set a boundary is to simply let people know your rules in a nonjudgmental way:

➡ I prefer not to talk on the phone during dinner, can I call you back?
➡ I would be happy to take turns cleaning up, but I don't want to be stuck doing it all by myself.
➡ I will not be taking my laptop with me on vacation.
➡ I get flustered when you raise your voice.

You can get away with stating personal preferences if you can do it without implied judgment or hostility. State it as a fact, like the sky is blue, as if it were the most natural, normal thing in the world.

Often the reason we hold back is that a personal preference may be paired with a judgment, and our initial impulse is to express the judgment. We know that we shouldn't go blurting *that* out—that would just alienate people. So instead of calling someone a lazy slob, you can request that they help you clean up. Instead of saying, "You heartless slave driver, you can't ask me to work on my vacation!" you can choose "I am planning to be out of reach on vacation."

You may not want to start by directly laying down the law. You may want to try something a little less authoritarian, like making a simple request:

➠ I get nervous when you raise your voice. It would help me a lot if you could lower it.

➠ I'm very frustrated and really need to vent. Could you hold off on the advice until I'm more ready to hear it?

➠ Please let me finish (my sentence, my point, another conversation).

➠ It doesn't work for me when you interrupt me in the middle of a phone call. Please let me finish my conversation.

Another, slightly softer touch is to ask a question exploring the possibility of a change in behavior and offer alternatives. The key is asking with a neutral tone:

➠ Would you consider placing your coffee cup someplace other than on my desk?

➠ Would you mind terribly turning down your music?

➠ Would you be willing to call before you come over in the future?

➠ Could we try doing things a little differently?

➠ May I ask a favor?

➠ I'd like to make a request.

➠ Could you help me out by . . .

It can be hard to acknowledge that a boundary you are setting might cause an inconvenience or sound a little odd. The only way to deal with this is just to tell the truth:

➠ I have a little idiosyncrasy you should know about . . .

➠ You may find this odd, but . . .

➠ I hate to cause an inconvenience, but this is very important to me. . . .

➠ Some people are a little surprised to know . . .

➠ I need to let you in on something about me that is a little out of the ordinary. . . .

➠ This is very personal and makes me feel a little uncomfortable but . . .

➠ This is embarrassing but . . .

➠ I want you to know . . .

4. **We might have to fight for the boundary, holding the line.**

It is reasonable to expect that most of the people in our lives will respect and honor the boundaries we set. Yet things aren't always that easy. What happens when people won't honor our "no fly zones"? Then we have the choice of caving in or holding the line. Most of the time we cave in, because holding our boundaries takes a concerted, deliberate effort.

There are three types of people who will refuse to honor a boundary:

The well intended but oblivious
The incapable
The bully

If a friend or colleague has agreed to observe a boundary but subsequently fails to do so, it is up to us to remind them of the agreement we made. Again in these instances, language often fails us. What we hear in our heads is often personal, reactionary, and not useful, such as calling someone who violates our boundaries an idiot or worse. We have to find other ways to point out that a boundary has been crossed. Options include:

It was my understanding that we had an agreement. Is that accurate? What can we do to make sure it is kept?

Do you remember the conversation we had about _____
_____ *? There seems to be a problem with what we*
agreed to. Can we discuss it?
We talked about this, and I must have misunderstood that you had
agreed to . . .
It is still important to me that you not _____ .
Could you remember in the future?

Variations on these options, though uncomfortable, should
work with the well intentioned. However, others will reveal their
inability to honor a boundary again and again over time, possibly
even over a period of years. With them you must make a choice:
you will either choose to tolerate the way this person violates
your boundaries or you will choose not to. You may decide to
limit your relationship by not sharing personal information or
spending time with them. The way many of us choose to be with
people, what we reveal or don't reveal to them, and the activities
we pursue in their company are all impacted by the boundaries
we can and cannot enforce with them. With some well-meaning
but incapable people we can just tell the truth:

My feelings are really hurt that you broke my confidence again. I
just don't feel safe sharing secrets with you.
I'd love to meet you for lunch, but I only have a half hour. I know
you can have challenges making places on time, so why don't we
make a dinner date that will allow us more flexibility on time.
I really enjoy your company, but it makes me awfully uncomfortable
to talk about other people in the department. Could we agree to
talk about our lives and the project?

Those who are truly incapable of respecting your boundaries simply need to go. Most of us just let relationships with these people

fade away—that is as good a way as any. But some boundary crossers pursue you and can force you to be blunt:

> *I have enjoyed some aspects of our relationship and feel we should*
> *focus on what works best about it.*
> *I prefer to spend my time a little differently.*
> *This doesn't work for me anymore.*

■ THE ENEMY AT WORK ■

Just as having a best friend at work can vastly increase job satisfaction, having an enemy at work is a leading source of stress. Not everyone has an enemy at work or someone they feel is "out to get them." But some people do and there is no getting around it. We wouldn't want to examine the concept of boundaries without addressing how to deal with bullies who simply won't respect perfectly reasonable ones.

We have all been tortured by someone who has decided to make our lives a misery. These include the neighbor who develops a fear and loathing for your cat and has extended it to you via nasty notes or the coworker who hates you on sight for no particular reason. The more we sense dislike or distrust from someone, the harder it is to set a boundary. We won't speculate as to what drives bullies, but standing up to them is the only way. The resentment that builds up when we allow bullies to have their way is a major source of stress that we can at least help you to manage.

It is one thing to set a boundary, get an agreement, and then have the agreement broken because of thoughtlessness. It is quite another to set a boundary and have it be denied. But what happens when we confront people and they say no? Then what? What if we don't have the authority to pull rank? The age-old specter of the playground bully looms large: "What are you going to do? Punch me?"

The pitched battles that play themselves out from row to row of cubicles in corporate America drain a lot of energy. These battles often result from a desire to exercise power or authority over others. Setting boundaries with bullies, or circling back and deciding what to do if they are denied, takes courage and shrewdness. Understanding the dynamics of power struggles can be an extremely useful thing.

In Chapter Four we referred to the Power Strategies Model. When you are dealing with a bully, especially one who has rank or a position of power over you, you are being dominated. As you may recall, when you are being dominated, four courses of action are available: submit, submerge, engage in open conflict, or commit sabotage. It would be fair to say that these are all ways of drawing a boundary.

As difficult as these four choices may appear, they are legitimate responses to domination. Before you engage in any of them, however, you may want to consider the following rules of battle.

First Rule. Choose your fights wisely and choose seldom. Pick your battles. If you decide to hold the line (e.g., pick a fight with a bully), make sure it is to advance or protect an issue of importance to you. If you engage in a fight because you just want to win on principle, you are signing up for untold heartache.

Second Rule. Take notes. Document behavior that is offensive and/or out of line. In work situations, documentation provides credibility in case a situation results in arbitration. This happens far more often than you might think. In personal situations, noting the facts can prevent your getting stuck in emotional responses and later give you the clarity you need to discuss events and how they made you feel.

Third Rule. Get professional help. The more you talk about the problem with people who can't help you, the more entrenched you will get in your point of view. You can vent, get a reality check, or strategize with friends or others, but if after all that talk you take no action, you are simply complaining. In work situations, your first recourse is your boss. After that there are often employee assistance programs or mediation services.

We know people who, when all else has failed, have left jobs or had themselves transferred because of bullies; removing themselves from the situation was the smartest thing they could do. Take your time, send out your résumé, build your exit strategy, but do it. If you are offered an exit interview, you can mention that a specific individual terrorized you. If yours is the only complaint, probably nothing will be done, but there is a good chance that you aren't the first.

In personal situations, getting help is equally important. Professional mediation, counseling, or therapy are all possible avenues to take if the suspected bully is important to you. If he or she is not a priority in your life, there is no question that you need to eliminate this bully from your life.

▣ THE GOOD NEWS ▣

We'd like to share a strange phenomenon that we have noticed. The real work around setting boundaries involves:

1. Getting clear about what the boundary is
2. Articulating the boundary, including practice runs when you say it out loud until you've got it down pat
3. Taking the plunge and being willing to set the boundary

Once this hard work has been done, you often don't need to say anything at all. There is a transfer of energy, psychic signaling, or some other indefinable magic that often occurs when the initial preparation is done. Suddenly the person with whom the boundary needs to be set simply stops the offending behavior. We don't know why this happens, but we've seen it time and again. A client is frustrated and upset about a specific person's behavior and works to identify, articulate, and role-play boundary-setting, finally committing to a time and place for a conversation with the offending party. But the very next day the person in question approaches them with an apology and a promise never to do it again. Or the offender just stops the behavior, giving the client no opportunity to say anything. It is uncanny. Is this just a coincidence? We don't think so. It is said that dogs smell fear, and in our opinion, people smell a pushover. If you know what your boundaries are and are ready to set them, there is a good chance people will sense it.

 ## Snapshot:

Georgia has a smile that could light a candle without a match. When she was in college her nickname was Sunshine, and that ultimately evolved into Sunny. In law school the nickname stuck, but when Georgia started work at her first law firm, she decided it was time to go back to her real, more professional-sounding name. She thought it would make a better impression. Her personality, however, had not changed; she was as warm and good-natured as ever. Her smile ignites easily and just won't quit.

Georgia was at the top of her law school class and has been assigned important cases by her law firm, but she is intimidated by the rough-and-tumble atmosphere of her firm. Meetings, even small ones, are a free-for-all; only the loudest and brashest attendees get heard. Georgia is overridden time and again not only by the senior partners but by just about everyone. She notices that others interrupt her at meetings and finish her statements for her, often taking credit for her insights or ideas. After three months of observation, taking notes on specific incidents that occur in meetings, it is clear to Georgia that a disturbing pattern has taken hold. Worse yet, she has begun to feel overwhelmed by the pack mentality; she knows she needs to stop this, but how?

Georgia realizes that she has to set clear boundaries that establish her right to be heard. She walks herself through the Three Perspectives—How do you see yourself? How do others see you? How do you want to be seen? Her written responses tell her there are problems at several levels.

The first question is how she sees herself. Does she believe she is worth hearing? Georgia asks herself to what extent she may have contributed to the problem by not wanting to seem rude or aggressive. She knows she is worth listening to; she has ample evidence from her years in law school, summer internships, and working with other strong-minded people on the law review.

Unfortunately, she concludes that others see her as not worth listening to, and that forces her to ponder how this has happened. She realizes that her image of herself as a nice person has kept her from standing up her for own ideas, thus allowing others to think that what she has to say has no value. After all, she realizes, if I am not willing to fight for airtime, why should someone do it for me?

As for how Georgia wants to be seen, she realizes that she wants to be seen as a player and that intellectually she is one. She also knows that to be effective in the firm, she is going to have to throw herself into the fray.

Georgia rehearses conversations with each individual who habitually interrupts her. The night before her self-designated "boundary day," she tosses and turns. She imagines John, one of the guys who started working at the firm at the same time she did, jeering at her and calling her a baby. She imagines one of the senior partners, a man who routinely curses at associates, letting loose at her with a string of choice expletives. Georgia nearly decides it's not worth the risk of total humiliation and considers abandoning the whole plan. After a night of little sleep, she gets out of bed, takes a cold shower, and figures it's better to fight and lose than to go down smiling politely.

At the next meeting, stomach roiling with distress, Georgia asks if she could add an item to the agenda. When it is her turn, she stands up and says: "Okay, here's the thing. You all constantly interrupt me."

Dan, a senior partner, immediately guffs, saying, "Oh, for crap's sake—"

"YOU ARE DOING IT RIGHT NOW," Georgia interrupts, a trickle of sweat seeping down the small of her back. Dan stops and looks around sheepishly. Georgia surveys the suddenly still room.

"You ask me questions but you don't let me answer. You don't listen to the questions I have. Worse, after I raise a point only to be overridden or interrupted, someone else makes the same point without interruption ten minutes later, getting the credit. Now I know you all respect me, because I get nothing but good feedback on my briefs, and every last one of you listens to me when we are speaking one on one. Not only that, many of you seek me out for help. Now I need your help. I need you to tell me what I am doing to create this. I am open to feedback. But I must change the way I am treated by everyone in this room."

Slightly stunned faces stare back at her. Surprisingly, only John, the fellow associate whose derision she'd so feared, is looking straight at her with a friendly look on his face. Everyone else looks shocked and uncomfortable. Georgia begins to suspect that she has made an irrevocable error. She remembers that she needs to offer alternatives.

"I also need to set up a signal that reminds you that you are interrupting, and I need you to give me permission to use it." The tension eases, yet there is still more silence. Then Dan takes a deep breath and says, "Okay, Georgia. What'll it be?"

Georgia and the group agree that when she is interrupted she will put her hand up, palm out. She goes on to make it plain that from that meeting on, she would request and expect that all involved let her finish her statements. That way the group could make decisions based on the in-depth information she was providing, and she would get credit for her ideas.

Did the interruptions stop? Not entirely. But Georgia had a way to deal with them. Did her method always work? No, in which case she would have to wave the hand, using her loudest voice to say "Please let me finish." What was most important was that Georgia had drawn a line and put herself at risk to hold it. Over time she realized that this earned her the respect of her associates and the partners.

Standing up for herself had yet another hidden benefit: Georgia's strength in stopping the interruptions and other railroading behavior in meetings inspired others to stand up for themselves as well. Over time the practice of letting others finish their points became standard. While meetings were often still raucous and heated, no longer were just a few loud voices driving each and every working session. Newcomers to the firm now learn early to use the hand, and most have no idea where it came from: the well-respected junior partner everyone calls Sunny.

■ WHAT DID GEORGIA DO? ■

1. Georgia recognized what she was tolerating and how that caused a boundary to be continually crossed.

2. She defined the exact nature of the boundary being violated.

3. She used the Three Perspectives to walk herself through all the angles she needed to get the whole picture and take responsibility for changing the situation. This she did by refusing to place blame on others for creating the problem or waste time complaining.

4. She owned her boundaries. She put a lot of thought into strategy and preparation.

5. She practiced the language she would use and had thought through alternatives for the things that were driving her nuts. She set up a contingency plan for herself so that she could name and claim what crossing the boundary looked and sounded like. Within the contingency plan was a bottom-line request that the group agree on an acceptable response.

What are you waiting for? Permission?

Forget it. None is forthcoming. If you feel like a victim in your relationships, look for the common denominator in each picture. If a boundary is consistently overrun, the only person who can fix it is you.

ONE UNORTHODOX SOLUTION: THE IMAGINARY NO-GUY

Movie stars have assistants and bodyguards to protect them from unwanted attention and requests. CEOs and senior executives have gatekeepers or hatchet people who screen calls and put people off. These are among the secret weapons of the rich and famous.

We know and love an influential author and speaker who has such a strong need to be liked and to make people feel great about themselves that he is incapable of saying no to anyone about anything. This is compounded by the fact that his curiosity and creativity are both great valuables to him. There are few ideas, projects, or people that do not turn him on or inspire him.

After years of trying everything, attempting the exercise of boundary-setting over and over, succeeding for a short time and then sliding back, our friend still suffered from an inability to say no, and it was running and ruining his life. The more successful he became, the more he was assailed with requests to which he unfailingly said yes! In time, the sheer mountain of services he was performing for others began to take its toll: his business colleagues feared for his health. His administrative assistants were harassed with the full-time job of trying to put people off and asking them to wait. Finally, he was assigned a full-time no-person. The no-guy literally followed our friend around and had an unequivocal reality-check conversation with the throng of people waiting in line for our friend's assistance in completing their projects. What a relief.

Most of us are not so popular that we need someone to keep the needy and adoring throngs at bay. But what if you were to pretend that you had a no-person who followed you around and questioned every commitment. What if you had a private secretary who knew your every move and lifted an eyebrow at you when you said yes instead of maybe or "Let me think about it"? What would be different?

Our hero from the beginning of this chapter, David, ended up building an imaginary no-person who became the arbiter of the way he allocated his precious time and resources. You can do the same. Pretend that you have an imaginary no-person who fights on your behalf. You would have to run every new thing you take on by this person. They would grill you on why you felt it was so important, how it would move you toward your Prime Objective, and what time on your calendar you were going to devote to it. They would ask you what the cost would be of overpromising on this new project and what the consequences would be. They would task you with responding to every new request (that was not a job requirement) with "Thank you for asking, let me think it through before I promise anything," so that you would in fact buy yourself some space and time to reflect appropriately. Your imaginary no-person will be the antidote to your already well-developed yes-person, the imaginary judge who drives you to be all things to all people all the time.

Exercise: **Boundaries**

This activity is designed to help you:

1. Define your boundaries
2. Put your boundaries into words and prioritize them
3. Identify potential obstacles and move beyond them
4. Draw your boundaries
5. Defend your boundaries

Start with one boundary and notice how it changes your quality of life. There are two ways to fail with this exercise:

1. Trying to set more than one boundary right away
2. Quitting when it gets scary

Step One: **Define your boundaries**

Think back to a time when you felt as if someone crossed a boundary. Remember a situation where you wished you had spoken up or been clearer about how you would prefer being treated. What happened? During or afterward, what did you feel?

What part of your body helped you to know that you were not being treated in accordance with your boundaries? (Did you get a headache, stomachache, or suddenly display cold or allergy symptoms?)

What were your thoughts? What did you say to yourself? What did you do?

What unspoken boundary had been violated? What is it that _____ did or said that specifically upset you? What kept you silent?

What was the boundary that was crossed?

_____

Step Two: **Refine your boundaries**

Finish the following sentences for yourself.

When I feel truly safe and productive, people do not (e.g., interrupt me, call me names, use foul language, tell me to shut up). (List at least five ways.)

1. _____

2. _____

3. _____

4. _____

5. _____

I feel truly respected and cared for when people do (e.g., let me finish my sentence, ask me how my day was, ask me how I feel, ask me what I think.) (List at least five ways.)

1. _____

2. _____

3. _____

4. _____

5. _____

Check the options that strike you as boundaries you might want to set:

Please don't interrupt me when I am on the phone.
Please don't call me at home unless I have specifically asked you to do so.
I don't answer the phone during dinner or after 10:00 P.M.
I don't work on Sundays.
I don't work after 10:00 P.M.
Please don't keep me waiting for too long.
Please don't yell at me unless your pants are on fire.
Please don't give me advice unless I ask for it.
Please don't expect me to do it your way.
Please don't try to manipulate me, just tell me what you think I need to know.
Please don't dredge up old grudges.

Please don't get personal.

When criticizing me, please focus on what is bothering you or on what needs to be changed and not on everything that is wrong with me.

Please do not comment on my appearance.

Please let me finish.

Please let me express my idea fully before shutting it down.

Please keep a reasonable physical distance between us.

I need you to listen to me without jumping in.

Please don't touch me.

Please don't hug me.

Please let me say no if that's what I need to do.

Write yours here:

_____

_____

_____

_____

_____

Remember: Once you have articulated a boundary very clearly in your own mind, it is often respected. Others often sense when a boundary is in place and act accordingly. You have taken the first step: defining your boundaries.

Step Three: **Prioritize**

Choose one boundary that you want to draw and articulate with a specific person that might significantly alter a situation for the better.

_____

_____

Step Four: **Remove self-imposed obstacles**

You have a fundamental right to be treated with respect. Many times others will behave toward you the way they feel comfortable being treated or just the way they feel like dealing with you at the moment. Often it is not personal and they simply need to be informed of your personal expectations. But first you must believe that it is in your best professional interest to be dealt with respectfully.

Think about the following:

➠ How will it help you to have clear boundaries?

➠ How will it help others if you have clear boundaries?

➠ How will you remember this when someone oversteps your boundaries?

➠ What keeps you from stating your boundaries?

Choose some of the reasons below or add your own:

➠ You do not feel that it is okay to have boundaries; you might appear inflexible or too high maintenance.

➠ You are afraid you will be punished (e.g., if you tell your bully of a supervisor that he cannot yell at you, you will be fired).

➠ You do not have the language; you don't know how to say it without appearing needy, whiny, or cold.

_____

_____

Even though setting boundaries with others is challenging, the cost of not setting them can be the loss of a relationship. More often than not, others would rather hear what is bothering you and make small shifts in their behavior than feel you slip away, never knowing why.

What will keep you from setting a boundary?

What mental shift will you make to work around your obstacle?

Who can you get to help you?

What would your imaginary no-person say or do?

Step Five: **Practice the language**

Often we fail to set and keep our boundaries because we do not have the language to articulate them.

We all know people who are really good at setting and communicating their boundaries clearly without turning people off. Everyone knows just how to treat them and does so. How do they communicate their boundaries?

Go back to the boundary you chose in Step Three. Choose a time to have a conversation with that person, and practice what you will say beforehand.

When?_____

What will you say?

(Practice with a friend first. Remember, just getting it out is helpful.)

Step Six: **Have the difficult conversation**

Once you've had the conversation, review what happened, so you can apply what you learned in the future. One thing to note is that, as uncomfortable as it may have been, no blood was shed. Everybody lived to see another day.

How did it go?
What went well?
What didn't go well?
What will you do again?
What will you do differently?
What did you learn?
What did the person you spoke with learn about you? About themselves?

Step Seven: **Own your boundaries**

Monitoring your boundaries and keeping the commitment to yourself is as hard as keeping weight off after a diet. Old habits die hard, and ancient behaviors creep back under stress. To fight the good fight, think about the following:

➡ How will you know when your boundaries have been overstepped?
➡ What will give you pause, so that you think, *Hmmm . . . this might be a boundary issue?*
➡ What will enable you to stop and articulate your boundaries with others before the situation becomes worse and relationships are impacted?
➡ How will you know when it's time to take the initiative and speak up?

Last thoughts about boundaries

We've made it sound simple, but we know it isn't and that there are a multitude of complicating factors. We can't tell you what yours will be, but we know that you'll have at least one because you are a complicated person in a complicated world. That is the constant *but* we hear from our clients.

> *"But you don't understand what a jerk this person is."*
> *"But you don't understand how important it is for me to be nice."*
> *"But you don't understand that my boss will fire me/assistant will hate me/friend will be mortally wounded. . . ."*
> *"But . . ."*
> *"But . . ."*
> *"But . . ."*

And here's the thing. You're right. That's the reason you haven't done it yet. And the question remains: what do you have to lose? Really?

- Knowing when and how to set boundaries properly will radically decrease your stress level.
- Setting boundaries can be uncomfortable at first.
- Setting good boundaries can become a habit. The smartest, best-adjusted people can still use a boundary upgrade.

CHAPTER TEN

Eliminate
Your Tolerations

What are you putting up with?

Tolerations are the seemingly inconsequential little things that drain away your energy. Thomas Leonard, a trailblazer in the coaching profession, coined the word to describe all the little stuff that takes up mental space and distracts us from the task at hand. Tolerations have a way of accumulating like barnacles on the hull of a ship. A few are not a problem, but layers of them seriously impede the vessel's speed and seaworthiness. What starts out as a hardly noticeable blip slowly becomes an annoying inconvenience, which over time turns into a major problem, undercutting productivity and happiness. Most people who have convinced themselves that they are disorganized or flaky are simply living and putting up with too many little problems.

 ## Snapshot:

Gina dashes into her office, late once again because of the slow elevator. How is it possible, she wonders, for a building this large to have so many incredibly slow elevators? An

engineer by trade, she knows the answer well: it's not the elevators, it's the volume of traffic. As she rushes to answer the phone for her 8:30 A.M. conference call, she nearly trips on a pile of books ("You've read all of these?" a friend who recently visited asked; the answer was yes). Pushing her stylish new glasses into place while blowing a stray strand of curly black hair out of her face, she throws herself into her chair, which makes its characteristic high-pitched squeak.

"What was that?" asks her potential new client.

"Oh, my office chair makes the funniest sound," Gina explains with a half-hearted chuckle.

The prospect gives a weak laugh, clearly not amused, and Gina makes yet another mental note to bring some WD-40 to the office tomorrow.

As she wraps up the call, Gina notices a slightly sour smell and discovers that once again the cleaning service has failed to dispose of the dead tulips on the coffee table. "I can't believe it! Do I need to do their job for them? Don't they notice? What do these people do anyway?" she asks aloud. She loves flowers, but the dead ones only remind her of her constant irritation with the building's janitorial personnel.

The potential client said that he would be sending her an overnight package. Immediately after they hang up, Gina remembers they need a special code on the FedEx packet because of the company's new mailroom procedures. She picks up the phone to call the prospective client back, then realizes that the number is in her electronic organizer, whose batteries have run down.

Her phone buzzes with an incoming call. That ringer is way too loud, Gina thinks for the umpteenth time. I have to get a new phone with a ringer that doesn't drive me crazy.

Gina lets the call forward to voice mail, making a mental note to retrieve it later, because the little light that indicates that she has messages burned out long ago. Her cell phone rings, and she silences the ringer when she sees it is her cousin Marcy, probably calling again to chat about her upcoming wedding. Gina has dropped several pointed hints *that talking during work hours is difficult, but Marcy doesn't get the message.*

Gina is a Stanford MBA with an advanced degree in engineering, known by her peers as both creative and brilliant and acknowledged as one of the top experts in her field. Yet all she can think right now is If anyone knew what a train wreck I am, they would never hire me. It is only 8:45 A.M. and Gina is already feeling hassled, annoyed, and drained. It's time to wake up and smell the tolerations.

Y ou might say that Gina has a valuable for an aesthetically pleasing environment that isn't being met, a need for things to be well engineered, or that she needs to draw a clear boundary with her cousin Marcy. You'd be right. In fact, recognizing what you are tolerating gives you the information you need to understand which Leverage Point to apply to eliminate the problem. This chapter helps you look from the big picture down to the tiniest detail to uncover what behaviors are getting in the way of your being your best possible self. And now is your chance to ditch them. A ship with too many barnacles requires more expensive fuel to get to port, but there is no amount of fuel that will help you to overcome your tolerations. Tolerations must be eliminated for you to have all the focus and energy you need to steam ahead toward your Prime Objective.

The details, as trivial as they appear to be, add up in such a way as to take up way too much of your precious brain space and time. One of the most famous examples of a small but exasperating toleration is found in the classic film *It's A Wonderful Life.* Jimmy Stewart constantly grabs the newel post at the bottom of the staircase in his house only to have the top come off in his hands. He is only slightly distracted by this the first time we see it happen; yet as things go increasingly awry and the stressors mount, he becomes more and more annoyed. Ultimately he dissolves into a completely irrational rage when the top of the post comes off yet one more time. We can all recognize ourselves in that progression. When his character comes back from his adventure of seeing what the world would have been like without him, the top of the post comes off in his hand *once again,* and he kisses it in recognition that his petty problems are nothing when compared to all that is good and wonderful about his life. It isn't an accident that this is one of the most popular movies of all time; we can all use the reminder. But if you can turn a toleration into something that reminds you how lucky you are, you are a rare being indeed. The rest of us are going to have to march off to the tool kit and hammer the darn top of the newel post down after throwing a little wood glue on there for good measure.

Let's find a few of your tolerations. There's nothing like seeing what you are up against to make the point that tolerations are something we must all reckon with on a regular basis.

Write down as many tolerations as you can think of as quickly as you can. Aim for at least twenty-five. Think about all the things that you are putting up with in your life, large and small. For example: no-fog mirrors that fog up, the hole in the pocket of your favorite jeans, the seven remote controls on your coffee table along with the mass confusion they cause (TV, VCR, DVD, stereo, cable), the person in your house who puts empty milk cartons back in the refrigerator (or leaves the full one on the counter to go sour), the calls you receive at dinner, commuter traffic, the dead lightbulb in the garage, the bad breath of your colleague at work, the coworker who listens to their voice mail on the speakerphone, dropped cell phone calls, technology problems of any kind—anything that bugs you in even the slightest way, anything that irks you again and again—often things not large enough to be real annoyances or dire enough to require your immediate attention, but things that just bug you anyway. Okay, start writing!

My Tolerations

1. _____
2. _____
3. _____
4. _____
5. _____
6. _____
7. _____
8. _____
9. _____
10. _____
11. _____
12. _____
13. _____
14. _____
15. _____
16. _____
17. _____
18. _____
19. _____
20. _____
21. _____
22. _____
23. _____
24. _____
25. _____

How many things did you write? What types of things came out? When most people do this for the first time it is usually quite a surprise. What is a surprise to you? How does this list make you feel? Are you simply interested, mildly upset, or do you feel like you've been hit by a truck? Are you relieved that nothing really big came up for you? Is there something on the list that makes you gasp? The first step in dealing with tolerations is naming them, so the good news is that you've already started the work of eliminating them. Near the end of this chapter we will take you through a more detailed exercise to help you deal with your tolerations once and for all—at least for now.

■ WHY DO WE HAVE TOLERATIONS ■ IN THE FIRST PLACE?

Wait a minute, you might be thinking, *I am a highly functional, organized adult; this is just way too elementary for me.* Not so. Think of tolerations this way. If you had to carry a marble in your pocket all day, it would probably not cause a problem. In fact, five or six marbles would only cause a slight inconvenience. However, many more than that would be a constant distraction, which might ultimately drive you nuts. It's the same with tolerations. A couple of them are not a big deal, but bunches of tolerations are noticeable. Having a significant number of tolerations will markedly reduce your quality of life. Tolerations also do not discriminate in terms of whom they affect. Even well-adjusted, extremely successful people have tolerations, often quite a few. Why? We accrue tolerations for the following reasons:

1. **We want to keep up a good attitude**. We don't recognize that we have them or how much they are bothering us. To admit we are tolerating a lot may feel like whining or complaining.

One of the biggest objections we get to making the tolerations list is "Why focus on the negative? I thought I was supposed to stay focused on the positive." Good point. We are not asking you to dwell on the negative, we are merely asking you to focus on what is *true* for you. Telling the truth about reality is not negative, it is common sense. Dwelling on tolerations and complaining about them without taking action would be negative. If tolerations are allowed to go unnoticed, they will multiply like mushrooms after a rainstorm. But also like mushrooms, they do not survive harsh light. To tell the truth about what's bugging you is not complaining, it is exposing your legitimate gripes to harsh light.

2. **It's too hard to get rid of them.** We feel it's going to take too much time, be too inconvenient, or cost too much money to eliminate our tolerations. Because the need to take care of tolerations is a constant, like maintaining your fitness level or caring for another, we are afraid that once we start down that road, it will never end. In fact, that's true. Like fitness, maintaining a toleration-free life is a *lifestyle*, a series of active, committed choices. The result of these consistent choices is a lot more energy to put toward what is important to you. Instead of focusing on how much it costs you to rid yourself of tolerations, you need to consider the cost of not taking care of them over the long run.

3. **We don't know how to get rid of them.** Sometimes a toleration is so big, or so overwhelming, that we can't imagine how to get rid of it. So we reconcile ourselves to powering through and living with it instead. The hold-your-breath-and-clench-your-jaw approach can get you through in the short term, but it's a tough act to keep up indefinitely.

4. **We feel that we don't deserve to address what we are tolerating or that we are not worth spending the necessary
   money on.** We feel that we should be selfless, more charitable,
   less demanding. This is connected to the First Perspective—how
   you see yourself—and the story you tell yourself about what you
   do and do not deserve. But we aren't talking about indulging
   your desire for a $136,000 sports car here, we are talking about
   small but substantial things that matter, like having the right
   stool in your bathroom so that you can sit down to put your
   sneakers on or having a coffee mug that fits the cup holder in
   your car for your morning commute. Do either of these things
   sound familiar? A lot of tolerations don't necessarily cost a lot of
   money to fix, but they do require that you choose to put a little
   focus, time, and energy into taking care of yourself. Again, the
   word *selfish* rears its ugly head. Yes, for you to be at your best, you
   must choose to be a little selfish.

Look at each of the items on your toleration list. Why have you
not taken care of them? Are they not your responsibility? Perhaps
you think they should be handled by your boss/colleague/spouse/
kid/employee? Do you not know where to turn to get the problem
fixed? Are some of the items just too small to deal with? Are some
too complicated for you to handle alone? Is there one so big that you
can't bear to think about it at all? Do you notice any patterns?

Tolerations exist for many different reasons and come in many
different forms. Some are just the cost of doing business, the things
that happen as the result of living. These tolerations must be taken
care of occasionally with the full understanding that they will return
again some day soon, like weeds in your lawn or dust bunnies under
the bed. Most in this area have to do with maintaining all the things
in our lives, especially those things with moving parts. We have
found that many people benefit greatly by setting aside a late night

at the office or a vacation day once every few months that they use to take care of the tolerations that have built up.

Some tolerations have to do with large issues in your environment. For example, we have a friend, Mark, who moved into a house after his divorce. It was an older and lower quality house than he had lived in when he was married. The house was full of tolerations, little and big things that needed fixing and replacing. Because the house was a respite after the trauma of living in a home full of conflict, it felt like a safe harbor for him, his own personal space, and the small problems it had were a part of its charm.

However, after eighteen months Mark started to notice those problems. He realized that he was living in a dump. One day the dishwasher broke and Mark snapped. He is now in the middle of a comprehensive renovation, and he's as pleased as can be. He may be dealing with residential contractors who rarely show up when they say they will, but he's happy.

Mark is surprised by the energy he finds in taking on his tolerations, but we aren't. Tolerations have a magical aspect, and when we acknowledge them and take care of them, our quality of life goes up instantly. It's not clear why we get energy from taking care of tolerations, even the smallest ones, but we do. Over the years we have received many, many calls from people who are getting a huge lift from taking care of things, especially for themselves.

■ TOLERATIONS IN RELATIONSHIPS ■

Relationships are dynamic, and over time they also develop tolerations. When we are tolerating things in our relationships, it generally means that a boundary is being violated, a standard is not being met, or we have allowed ourselves to get into a relationship with someone whose valuables conflict with ours. Obviously, dealing with tolerations in our relationships takes more care and thought than changing the porch light, but the concept remains the same. These tolerations occur because we do not take care of what bothers us as it happens—often a crossed boundary—and this allows irritations to build up over time, resulting in deeper problems. When we fail to attend to the tolerations in our relationships, resentment is sure to build up, and as we noted in the previous chapter, resentment always hurts a relationship. Once we recognize that we resent another person, we must find a way to release the resentment we are carrying as well as find a way to deal with the action or behavior we are tolerating.

When tolerations reach a critical mass we must make a choice: we either have to invest in fixing the relationship or end it. It is a fact of life that we can outgrow our relationships and then must reinvent them or simply end them. Sometimes the people in our lives cannot or will not help us do what we must do to reach our Prime Objective. It sounds harsh, but eliminating draining or unsupportive people from your life will positively impact the quality of your life in ways you cannot imagine.

 Snapshot:

Sara has a busy and complicated life. For the past fifteen years she has been the president of an architectural design company she founded with a small group of colleagues. Since its founding, the company has grown from a small operation with ten employees to a nationally recognized firm of over two hundred and fifty employees. In addition to her career, she and her husband, John, who is also a senior designer with the firm, have raised two children and have maintained a relationship that everyone in their life admires.

How has she done it? Sara has had a secret weapon for the past fifteen years—her family assistant and house manager, Nancy. Sara has been able to focus on her business, be a great mom, and have a successful marriage largely because Nancy has taken care of the details at home.

Are clients coming over for dinner? No problem, Nancy will get it catered.
Is John's mother visiting for a month? No problem, Nancy will help her get around town and take care of the details of her stay, even organizing a weekly appointment at a local hairdresser. Is the garbage disposal on the fritz? No problem, Nancy is there to meet the repairman.

Sara hired Nancy to take care of her, especially in the elimination of tolerations and management of the countless details of a thriving household. So what is Sara's toleration? Unfortunately, the toleration is Nancy herself. All of a sudden (or was it?), Nancy has become a source of stress. Nancy always had some strange ways about her, little idiosyncrasies like a slightly rigid way of going about things. She would miss an occasional detail or get huffy about someone completing a task she had started in a way that was not up to her standard. Everyone accepted those quirks as "just Nancy," after all, she's only human. Sara was able to overlook these little things because Nancy was reliable, honest, and most of all, she cared for the family.

Then Sara realized one day that the relationship with Nancy had turned sour and that she was tolerating it. The list of negatives had grown to a point where they outweighed the positives, and recently Sara had found it increasingly difficult to confront Nancy about what wasn't working. For years they had had a rhythm between them—dealing with problems was easy and nonconfrontational. Now somehow things had shifted, and Nancy was increasingly defensive and hostile. Sara found that she was avoiding Nancy, causing increased communication snafus that only exacerbated the tension. Sara had a problem on her hands, and she needed to get the working relationship back on track or find a replacement.

After several attempts to confront Nancy and reset expectations, it became clear that there was no use trying to repair the relationship. Once Sara came to that realization, her stress skyrocketed. Nancy had been there for fifteen years, since the kids were toddlers. How could she get rid of her now? Not only did Nancy know every detail of the household, but she was like a member of the family, the kids loved her, even the neighbors loved her.

It took Sara and her husband a few weeks to decide how and when to ask Nancy to leave. When it was time to let her go, it was just as painful as they thought it would be, gut-wrenching in fact, and yet it was worth it. Now every day when Sara walks into her house after a long day's work, she is happy and peaceful. Her new assistant, Jennifer, takes care of everything to perfection, and she is a delight to deal with.

Sometimes you must upgrade the relationships in your life and proactively surround yourself with people who will help you achieve the life you want rather than impede your progress. One of the essential lessons of coaching is that you have choice; you can choose what you will and will not tolerate. It can seem heartless, but you can choose whom you will or will not include in your life.

■ TAKING BACK CONTROL ■

One of our favorite stories is about Scott's father, Ken Blanchard. A few years ago Scott arranged for his father to work with a coach to help him deal with some issues that he was continually facing, mostly centered around the personal cost of having too many demands placed on his life. There was always so much to do—so many places to be, too many people to see.

A few weeks after Ken started with his coach a very funny thing occurred. During a break in an important board of directors meeting, Ken dragged Scott and a couple of board members out to his car. He wanted to show them something extraordinary. Ken opened up the trunk and, smiling from ear to ear, showed everyone that he had cleaned it out for the first time in years. Ken had always been an incredibly creative leader, author, and speaker while not being especially neat or organized. Ken was a pack rat with a legendarily messy study filled with one of the greatest collections of piles of paper, all important, anyone had ever seen.

Ken was excited because he had identified and eliminated a toleration: his messy trunk. It was the beginning. Over the next few months, Ken moved beyond clearing up tolerations to dealing with some of the larger issues in his life, such as being overcommitted and overwhelmed. He has lost thirty-five pounds, created a more effective staff with the discipline to protect him from too many commitments, and he has begun to say no without guilt.

■ NOT EVERYTHING CAN BE FIXED ■

There are tolerations that cannot be fixed. We all have to deal with a certain amount of misfortune or inconvenience; no one is exempt from that. Extremely difficult tolerations are what is left over in life that we simply do not have control over—a loved one who is ill who takes a lot of time and energy, a certain amount of noise on city streets, traffic.

But even tolerations that can't be eliminated might be managed more effectively. Just because we are stuck with something doesn't mean we can't find a way to make the best of it.

Intractable tolerations are often caused because we have chosen to get a need—like duty—met or to do something that is perfectly aligned with our valuables—like to care for others. These show up most often in our personal lives and are usually the result of the choice to make a sacrifice on someone else's behalf. The operative word is *choice*—you always have a choice, even when it sometimes doesn't feel that way. An example of this is a woman who can't stand the mess her fiancé's ancient, beloved dog makes in the house they share. She accepts the dog because she loves her intended, but that doesn't mean that they can't reach some compromises about how to handle the situation.

The key with seemingly intractable tolerations is to break them down into their smallest possible components and see what might be done about the small pieces. Once that is done, you can question assumptions you might have made about having to accept things exactly the way they are. For example, while it may be true that the dog must be loved and cared for, there is no law that says it must have free run of the house. Perhaps it can be limited to only certain parts of the house that are designated dog areas.

If you are someone who rails against the traffic that you have to deal with where you live, it's true—you can't change that. But you can change your response to it: you can leave earlier, you can schedule conference calls to make good use of the time, you can listen to tapes and catch up on your reading or even learn a new language! There are some things we cannot change, but we can always change our attitude.

■ THE TOLERATIONS EXERCISE ■

Ditch your tolerations once and for all.

In the beginning of this chapter you created a quick list of your tolerations. In the following exercise we will go deeper into your tolerations and develop concrete actions you can take today to radically increase the quality of your life. The delightful thing about listing your tolerations is that some of them will take care of themselves the minute you flush them out.

Use this exercise:

1. When the Scrubdown indicates that you are putting up with a lot of little details and are being drained.

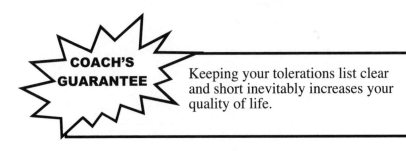

COACH'S GUARANTEE Keeping your tolerations list clear and short inevitably increases your quality of life.

2. When everything big in your life is going extremely well (relationships, career), but you find yourself out of sorts and cranky.

3. Every spring for a "spring cleaning," whether you think you need it or not.

Tolerations Identification

Go through the different areas of your life and use this list to jog your thinking regarding what is bugging you.

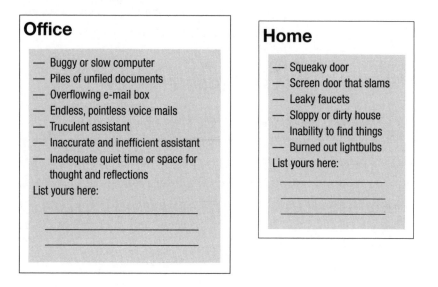

Office

— Buggy or slow computer
— Piles of unfiled documents
— Overflowing e-mail box
— Endless, pointless voice mails
— Truculent assistant
— Inaccurate and inefficient assistant
— Inadequate quiet time or space for thought and reflections
List yours here:

_____
_____
_____

Home

— Squeaky door
— Screen door that slams
— Leaky faucets
— Sloppy or dirty house
— Inability to find things
— Burned out lightbulbs
List yours here:

_____
_____
_____

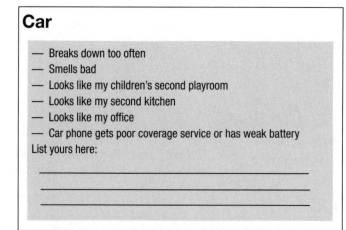

Car

— Breaks down too often
— Smells bad
— Looks like my children's second playroom
— Looks like my second kitchen
— Looks like my office
— Car phone gets poor coverage service or has weak battery
List yours here:

_____
_____
_____

Relationships

— Friends or relatives who berate, criticize, or judge constantly
— Friends or relatives who are late and don't call
— People who take you for granted
— People who expect certain things
— People who manipulate
— Those who cannot apologize even when you know they know they are wrong

List yours here:

_____

_____

_____

‡ Wardrobe

— Never have the right thing on hand
— Hate my clothes
— Shoes need to be reheeled
— Don't have the right shoes, socks, stockings for the outfit
— Forget to pick up dry cleaning
— Clothes no longer fit

List yours here:

_____

_____

_____

Miscellaneous

— Travel
— Pets
— Shoddy professionals
— Poor service

List yours here:

_____

_____

_____

▨ TRIAGE AND ORGANIZATION ▨

1. Place an asterisk next to all the tolerations that you can eliminate on your own.

2. Place a D next to all the tolerations that you can ask someone else to handle. (These then get transferred to the delegate box.)

3. Place a P next to all the tolerations you can pay someone else to handle. Don't worry if you can't afford it.

4. Place an E next to all the tolerations that you can simply eliminate.

5. Place an NS next to all the tolerations that seem intractable and do not fit into any other category. This is the place that you put those items for which you believe there are no solutions whatsoever and that you are resigned to having to live with.

■ TROUBLESHOOTING AND ACTION PLANNING ■

Delegate

Who might you ask to help you with this?

How will you inspire them to help you?

How will you be sure it gets done?

How will you follow up?

By what date will you have this handled?

Items	Actions: Who?/What?/How?	By When?/Follow-Up

▪ PAY SOMEONE ▪

Paying for help is not something everyone can afford. One reason for this is that when people create their budgets, they don't plan for things to break or wear out. It takes a certain kind of temperament and/or maturity to plan for maintenance costs of anything you own. If this is the case for you, the biggest favor you can do for yourself is to start a tolerations fund and begin budgeting 5 percent of your income to take care of the small stuff. This may mean foregoing a nice new TV or some evenings out, but taking care of tolerations is something you need for your quality of life and should be put ahead of the things you want.

Some simply live on the financial edge, which means that they will have to be extra creative about getting tolerations handled. If this is the case, think about how you might do a trade with someone who can help you.

1. If you have enough income to cover it, work through the following; if not, skip down to 2.
   - What has kept you from taking care of this? (E.g., I need to have someone come to the house and I am always at work.)
   - What steps do you need to take to remove the obstacle? (E.g., set a date two months from now when I will take a vacation day to stay home to deal with all the different professionals who will come and take care of the problems in my house.)
   - How much does it bother you?
   - What kind of professional do you need?
   - What do you need to do to find the right kind of professional?
   - By what date will you have done the research? Hired the right person? Completed the job?

2. If money is too tight to hire someone, work through this one.

⟹ Whom do you know who has the expertise you need and who might be able to help you?

⟹ Can you barter or trade services with this person?

Or—make a short list of tolerations with an estimate of what it might cost to handle them, and ask friends and relatives to give you the elimination of that toleration instead of gifts for special holidays.

Or—begin a tolerations fund and slowly save up to create the finances to deal with your tolerations.

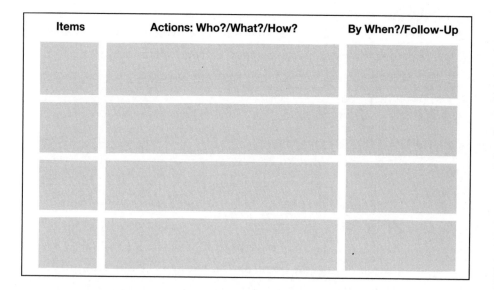

Items	Actions: Who?/What?/How?	By When?/Follow-Up

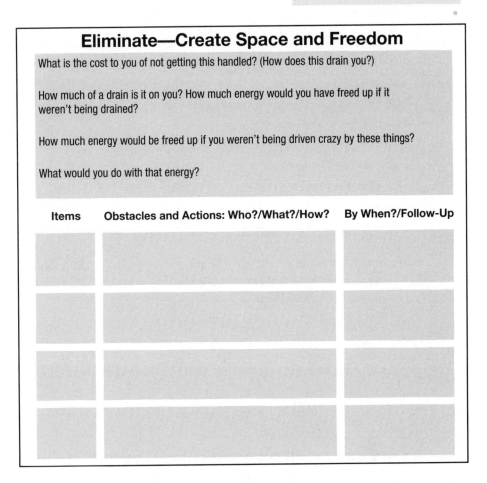

Eliminate—Create Space and Freedom

What is the cost to you of not getting this handled? (How does this drain you?)

How much of a drain is it on you? How much energy would you have freed up if it weren't being drained?

How much energy would be freed up if you weren't being driven crazy by these things?

What would you do with that energy?

Items	Obstacles and Actions: Who?/What?/How?	By When?/Follow-Up

Remember, tolerations are a part of life. They build up naturally over time and must be dealt with on a regular basis. The power of tolerations comes from their buildup and from their subsequent removal. Sometimes the best thing you can do for your state of mind is to literally change a lightbulb in the hallway, clean out your file drawer, or get the hem fixed on your favorite pants. Dealing with tolerations has a magical way of putting a spring back in your step so you can get back to the business you are most needing to focus on!

■ NO SOLUTIONS ■

The "no solutions" tolerations—reexamine and choose another attitude.

What are you tolerating that cannot be changed?

What bothers you so much about it?

1. _____

2. _____

3. _____

Is there anything you might change about one or two of these details?

Ask yourself:

➡ If I could wave a magic wand, what would be different about this situation?

➡ What assumptions have I made that lead me to believe that this situation is unchangeable?

➡ If I were someone different, someone who had not made this assumption, what might I do to change this situation?

➡ If a friend were in this situation, what would I advise him or her to do?

➡ If a friend were in this situation, how would I let him or her "off the hook" in a way that I do not allow myself?

Items	Assumptions-Actions: Who?/What?/How?	By When?/Follow-Up

Tolerations—Master List

Items	Delegate, Pay, Eliminate, NS—Examine and Choose	Obstacle and Action	By When?

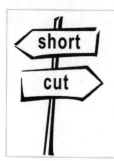

- During the tolerations process you will gain clarity about what you can change and what you can't.
- Listing what you are putting up with doesn't make you a whiner; it is the beginning of the process of eliminating what drains you.
- Eliminating tolerations prevents your being distracted from what is really important.

CHAPTER ELEVEN

Almost Perfect

Snapshot:

John, whom you may remember from Chapter One, is driving along the highway having left work at 6:00 P.M. He is listening to a novel on tape—a new habit he picked up to make his commute less stressful. If he must do a meeting on a cell phone, he will, but he usually designates this drive as "his." He is listening to a story about a character who is simply miserable—working too hard, harangued by his wife, estranged from his kids. A year ago he would have described himself that way. He smiles and thinks to himself, Well, I could give him a few pointers.

First, he thinks, that guy needs to understand what makes him so good at what he does and why he is valuable to his company. This guy has to have a heart-to-heart with his boss about how to best leverage himself and keep from burning out. He's got to understand what he needs to do his best work and make sure he gets it from the people around him. Then he has to set some boundaries with his colleagues, his team members, and at home.

John remembers the first conversation he had with his family about what was most important to him and how surprised he was listening to what they said about what was important to them. He still feels the intense relief of making promises he felt he could keep and planning family events that everyone could enjoy.

He grins when he thinks of the surprised look on his wife's face when he sat down with her and said, "What are you putting up with, and how are we going to make things right? Let's figure this out together." He discussed the pressures at work and made clear agreements about when he would be home that would ease some of the unspoken resentment and pressures.

John knows that he has to stay vigilant—that the respect he's earned from his boss and his team, not to mention the ease he has achieved at home, is not to be taken for granted. But for now, he feels content, like the architect and master of his own life. He is pleased and grateful. He feels . . . well . . . perfect. Or close enough.

ACKNOWLEDGMENTS

For this book we really have to thank our agent, Margret McBride. It was her idea, and her enthusiasm for the material, her relentless encouragement, and her thoughtful feedback were a huge factor in getting some of the more complex ideas across. We will never forget when we started to get it right and she literally danced around her office. Margret believed in our ideas and us, and we are deeply touched and grateful. Big thanks also to Henry Ferris, our editor, who put so much time and energy into making this book clear and readable. His ability to put himself in the reader's shoes and challenge us to explain it better is uncanny. Henry went way above and beyond the call of duty for this book.

A number of friends read early versions and gave us valuable feedback. Amy Solas, Marjorie Miller, Chris Edmonds, Ken and Margie Blanchard, thank you for your valuable comments and giving us your precious time. Thank you to Martha Lawrence, editor extraordinaire, who took time out of an already packed schedule to offer invaluable help and desperately needed support. Finally, Jennifer Boyd, thanks from the bottom of our hearts for swooping in at the last minute with a smile on your face and the world's best attitude to apply your masterful skill to making our work look so grand!

MADELEINE

Thomas Leonard, mentor, teacher, and sand in my oyster, said, "Anything worth doing is worth getting help with." Of all the things he taught me (there were a lot) that one caused the most radical shift. I get a lot of help now, so I have a lot of people to thank:

Henry Kimsey-House, my first coach, who guided me to find my calling, my gift, and my passion. Belle-Linda Halpern, a dear friend, and her partner at the Ariel Group, Kathy Lubar, who gave me my first opportunity to teach coaching skills to managers back when it was a novel idea. Belle and Kathy taught me instructional design, how to train and work in organizations—down to how to dress appropriately. They gave me feedback even when it was hard. They were patient, generous, and kind, always.

My coaches—Dana Morrison, Shirley Anderson, David Goldsmith, William Pilder. Thanks for helping me keep me eye on the ball and for helping me dust myself off the many times I fell down.

My talented partner at Coaching.com, Linda Miller, whose loving way, sense of humor, and tireless pull forward have been a tremendous source of energy.

A coach is nothing without clients; all the training programs in the world and mentors aside, my clients really taught me how to coach. I thank you for showing up, doing your homework, keeping a sense of humor, and going farther than you thought you could. You are all in this book, and as you can see, you continue to inspire me long after you have moved on.

Even as clients get coached, businesses get run, and books get written, life goes on. I am deeply grateful to the people I love who help me squeeze the last precious drop out of each day. Laura

Berman Fortgang, my dearest pal in the crazy quest to have it all and in juggling the madness when it all comes at once! My wise women, Leslie Mason, Britt Louise Gilder, and Marjorie Miller, who laugh at me and with me. My sister, Mia Homan, who really should be running the world—her competence and passion touch everyone near her. Mia was my first editor and has been a constant source of support ever since I can remember. My partner in parenting, and in some of the harder life lessons, John Hickok, I thank for being a prince among men. Also our beautiful, wise, witty, and loving children, Hannah and Atticus, for putting up with their mom's need to accomplish.

Finally, my partner in business, writing, and fun, fun, fun, Scott, thank you for your brilliant mind, your generosity of spirit, and your ebullient sweet nature.

SCOTT

I must first acknowledge Laura Berman Fortgang, as she was the first coach I met. LBF introduced me to everyone she knew in coaching, most importantly my coauthor, Madeleine Homan. I also would like to acknowledge those coaches who took an interest in my quest to understand coaching during my first ICF conference, John Seiffer and Heather Davis.

You never forget your first coach, and none is better than Jaye Myrick. Jaye was the first person in my life who was truly at service to me with no agenda other than my personal success.

I owe a big thank-you to my current coach, Stephen Cluney, whose insightful comments led us to the title for this book.

I would like to thank my pals from the early days at Coaching.com, Chip Bruss, Vicki Halsey, Jamie Grettum, Debbie Zaleschuk, Joni Wickline, Linda Miller, Pamela Logan, Howard Farfel, Charlotte Jordan, and, of course, our wonderful coaches.

A special thanks to our first big client and the people who believed in our vision of democratizing coaching, Jay Crookston, Mark Bersani, and Kathy Viverka. Also special thanks to our first multiyear client, Spence Nimberger at PGI in Houston.

Special thanks to everyone at The Ken Blanchard Companies who has supported our investment in coaching. Special thanks to Uncle Tom McKee for his faith in me.

Thanks to my kids and former wife, Chris Blanchard, for the patience and support this book has demanded from each of you.

And finally, heartfelt thanks to my partner extraordinaire, Madeleine Homan, the bubbles in my champagne, who has been my business partner, friend, coach, copresenter, and now coauthor. Without you, Madeleine, life would not be the same.

FURTHER READING

COACHING

Coaching for Leadership; Marshall Goldsmith, Laurence Lyons, and Alyssa Freas; Jossey-Bass/Pfeiffer, 2000.

Coaching for Performance; John Whitmore; Nicholas Brealy Publishing, 1992.

Co-Active Coaching: New Skills for Coaching People Toward Success in Work and Life; Laura Whitworth, Henry Kimsey-House, and Phil Sandahl; Davies-Black, 1998.

The Handbook of Coaching: A Resource Guide to Effective Coaching with Individuals and Organizations; Frederick Hudson; Hudson Institute Press, 1998.

Masterful Coaching; Robert Hargrove; Jossey-Bass/Pfeiffer, 2000.

The Heart of Coaching; Thomas Crane; FTA Press, 1998.

The Portable Coach: 28 Surefire Strategies for Business and Personal Success; Thomas Leonard and Byron Larsen; Scribner's, 1998.

Take Yourself to the Top: The Secrets of America's #1 Career Coach; Laura Berman Fortgang; Warner Books, 1998.

BUSINESS AND LEADERSHIP

The E-Myth Revisited; Michael E. Gerber; Harper Business, 1995.

The Fifth Discipline; Peter M. Senge; Doubleday, 1990.

First, Break All the Rules; Marcus Buckingham and Curt Coffman; Simon & Schuster, 1999.

Good to Great; Jim Collins; Harper Business, 2001.

Leadership and The One Minute Manager; Ken Blanchard, Patricia Zigarmi, and Drea Zigarmi; William Morrow, 1985.

The Leadership Pill; Ken Blanchard and Marc Muchnick; Simon & Schuster, 2003.

On Becoming a Leader; Warren Bennis; Addison-Wesley Publishing, 1989.

Servant Leadership: A Journey into the Nature of Legitimate Power and Greatness; Robert K. Greenleaf; Paulist Press, 1997.

Shackleton's Way: Leadership Lessons from the Great Antarctic Explorer; Margot Morrell, Stephanie Capparell, and Alexandra Shackleton; Penguin, 2002.

IMPROVED COMMUNICATION AND RELATIONSHIPS

Difficult Conversations: How to Discuss What Matters Most; Douglas Stone, Bruce Patton, and Sheila Heen; Penguin, 1999.

Fierce Conversations; Susan Scott; Viking Press, 2002.

"How Bell Labs Creates Star Performers"; Robert Kelley and Janet Caplan; *Harvard Business Review*, July/August, 1993.

The One Minute Apology; Ken Blanchard and Margret McBride; William Morrow, 2003.

Primal Leadership; Daniel Goleman, Richard Boyatzis, and Annie McKee; Harvard Business School Press, 2002.

Whale Done; Ken Blanchard, Thad Lacinak, Chuck Tompkins, and Jim Ballard; William Morrow, 2002.

Leadership Presence; Belle-Linda Halpern and Kathy Lubar; Gotham Books, 2003.

ESTABLISHING PRIME OBJECTIVES

Callings: Finding and Following an Authentic Life; Gregg Michael Levoy; Three Rivers Press, 1997.

In Transition; Mary Lindley Burton; Harper Business, 1992.

Now What? Laura Berman Fortgang; Tarcher-Penguin, 2004.

The Purpose Driven Life: What on Earth Am I Here For?; Rick Warren; Zondervan, 2002.

The Soul's Code: In Search of Character and Calling; James Hillman; Warner Books, 1996.

What Color Is Your Parachute? Richard Nelson Bolles; Ten Speed Press, 1983.

What Should I Do with My Life? Po Bronson; Random House, 2002.

GIFTS

The Four Fold Way: Walking the Paths of the Warrior, Teacher, Healer and Visionary; Angeles Arrien; HarperCollins, 1993.

Now Discover Your Strengths; Marcus Buckingham and Donald Clifton; Free Press, 2001.

Soar with Your Strengths; Donal O. Clifton and Paula Nelson; Dell, 1992.

NEEDS

Gifts Differing: Understanding Personality Type; Isabel Briggs Myers and Peter B. Myers; Consulting Psychologists Press, 1997.

Motivation and Personality; Abraham Mazlow; Harper & Row, 1970.

Please Understand Me; David Keirsey; Prometheus Nemesis Books, 1998.

Portraits of Temperament; David Keirsey; Prometheus Nemesis Books, 1987.

Understanding Yourself and Others; Linda V. Berens; Telos Publications, 1998.

VALUABLES

Attitudes, Beliefs and Values; Milton Rokeach; Jossey-Bass, 1968.

Managing by Values; Ken Blanchard and Michael O'Connor; Berrett-Koehler Publisher, 1997.

BOUNDARIES

Healing the Shame That Binds You; John Bradshaw; Health Communications, 1988.

Learning to Say No: Establishing Healthy Boundaries; Carla Will-Bernadon; Health Communications, 1990.

No Is a Complete Sentence; Megan LeBoutillier; Ballantine Books, 1995.

ON BECOMING A COACH

Coaching is such a wonderful profession that it naturally attracts thousands of service-oriented people who are thrilled to find a career in which they can fully leverage what they are best at.

If you recognize yourself as a "natural coach," please go to the International Coach Federation for information. The ICF is a not-for-profit organization devoted to serving professional coaches and their clients. The ICF certification process is rigorous but worth the effort.

14441 I Street, N.W., Suite 700
Washington, D.C. 20005
Phone: 888-423-3131 (main office) or 888-236-9262
   (coach referral service)
Web site: www.coachfederation.org

There are many outstanding training programs. The ones we know and can therefore recommend are:

Corporate Coach U International (CCUI)

Coach University

The Coaches Training Institute

Georgetown University Center for Professional Development

The Hudson Institute of Santa Barbara

New Ventures West

The Newfield Network

International MOZAIK

If you are already a professional certified coach and are interested in working with us at The Ken Blanchard Companies, please, visit our Web site at www.coaching.com. Go to the "How to contact us" section and fill out the coach application. We go into recruiting mode occasionally, and filling out the application is the best way to stay on file with us. Please do not call our offices or send a hard copy résumé. We love technology and prefer to use it to stay in touch and organized!

SERVICES AVAILABLE

The Ken Blanchard Companies is a global leader in workplace learning, employee productivity, and leadership effectiveness. Through seminars and in-depth consulting in the areas of teamwork, customer service, leadership, performance management, and organizational change, The Ken Blanchard Companies helps people learn—and coaching specifically ensures that people apply their learning to their day-to-day jobs. Blanchard's acquisition of Coaching.com in 2002 placed the company on the map as a leading provider of coaching services. Blanchard now offers an array of coaching services and training programs that have been designed to specifically address the biggest challenges facing organizations and their leaders today. These include organizational changes; broad learning initiatives; individual coaching of managers, professionals, and executives; and Coaching Essentials for Leaders, a coaching skills program to help individuals become more effective, coachlike leaders.

To learn more about Blanchard's high-impact training and coaching programs, visit the Web site or contact the company directly at:

The Ken Blanchard Companies

125 State Place

Escondido, CA 92029

Phone: 800-728-6000 or 760-489-5005

Fax: 760-489-8407

Web sites: www.kenblanchard.com and www.coaching.com

ABOUT THE AUTHORS

MADELEINE HOMAN, MCC

Ms. Homan is the vice president of Blended Solutions at The Ken Blanchard Companies. She is a founder of Coaching.com and an author of the Internet platform used to support large coaching initiatives. With more than fourteen years of experience as a master certified coach (MCC), Madeleine was instrumental in developing the core curriculum for Coach University where she was a senior trainer and is the designer and facilitator of The Manager as Coach, which is the core coaching curriculum for several companies worldwide. She is also an author of The Ken Blanchard Companies coaching skills course: Coaching Essentials for Leaders.

Madeleine has been a pioneer in the coaching profession and has served as the president of Straightline Coaching, a founding advisory board member and senior trainer for Coach University, and a founding board member for the International Coach Federation, on whose board she served for six years.

Ms. Homan's expertise in business coaching has been highlighted on ABC, NBC, CBS, and Fox News Channel. Her presence in the marketplace extends into press articles in *The New York Times, London Times, Training & Development Magazine, ASTD Publications,* and *Women's Media.* She splits her time between Dobbs Ferry, New York, and Escondido, California.

SCOTT BLANCHARD

Scott Blanchard is an accomplished speaker, trainer, and organizational consultant, well versed in leadership, teamwork, coaching, customer service, and organizational strategy.

In 1999 Scott founded Coaching.com, a business dedicated to the democratization of coaching in organizations. Coaching.com has coached over three thousand clients. In 2002 Coaching.com was acquired by The Ken Blanchard Companies, an internationally recognized management and leadership training and consulting firm based in San Diego, California.

Scott is currently the executive director of service delivery at The Ken Blanchard Companies. As a family member and part owner of The Ken Blanchard Companies, Scott represents the "next generation" charged with leading the business into the future.

Scott lives on top of Bernardo Mountain in beautiful Escondido, California.